Fishing the Hauraki Gulf

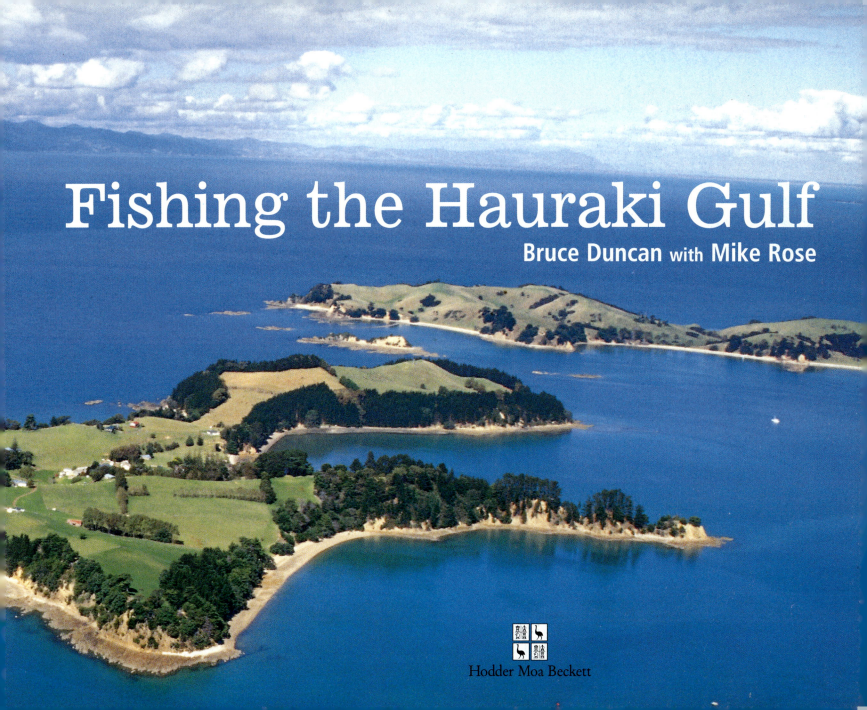

Fishing the Hauraki Gulf

Bruce Duncan with Mike Rose

Hodder Moa Beckett

National Library of New Zealand Cataloguing-in-Publication Data
Duncan, Bruce, 1954-
Fishing the Hauraki Gulf/Bruce Duncan with Mike Rose.
ISBN 1-86958-931-9
1. Saltwater fishing — New Zealand — Hauraki Gulf.
I. Rose, Mike, 1957- II. Title.
799.16099332 — dc 21

ISBN 1-86958-931-9

Published in 2002 by Hodder Moa Beckett Publishers Limited
[a member of the Hodder Headline Group]
4 Whetu Place, Mairangi Bay, Auckland

Charts courtesy of the New Zealand Hydrographic Office
Illustrations by Andreena Buckton, Noodle Design Corp.

Designed and produced by Hodder Moa Beckett Publishers Limited
Scanning by Microdot, Auckland
Printed by Printlink, Wellington

To Jim and Jean Duncan and Inge and Cyril Rose for the priceless early encouragement and all those fantastic experiences; to Alison and Dorte, for simply putting up with us; to Jack and Rudi for all the laughter and fun times — and to the Hauraki Gulf, our wonderful, unique playground.

The authors would like to thank the following:

Contents

Introduction

The Hauraki Gulf is New Zealand's most popular fishery. Its snapper-laden waters lap the shores of both our biggest city and the literally dozens of townships and communities that lie along its edges.

Although the Gulf is home to many species of fish, the focus of this book is snapper. Although we occasionally refer to other species such as kahawai, kingfish and John Dory, *Fishing the Hauraki Gulf* is primarily about catching snapper — how to do it better and where to go. As well as lots of practical tips, we have also included over 200 proven spots — a small fraction of the places where snapper can be caught in the Hauraki Gulf. As your knowledge and experience grows, you will quickly add many more to your own personal database.

The Hauraki Gulf is a huge and diverse area and, although we have included some of the more remote areas, we have concentrated mainly on spots closer to home, those that are easily reached by even quite small runabouts. Sadly, this has meant there is no room for that most majestic of Hauraki Gulf islands, Great Barrier. An incredible fishing habitat, the Barrier easily warrants 200 spots on its own. It may have to be the focus of the next book . . .

Bruce Duncan has been fishing the waters of the Hauraki Gulf since he was a young boy in the late 1950s. Born and raised in the Auckland eastern suburb of St Heliers, he learnt to fish at a young age and was soon pulling snapper from the nearby reef structures and rocks. He caught his first snapper with his bare hands in a rock pool . . .

As a teenager, Bruce 'ran away to sea', setting sail on the Nathan's offshore keeler, *Kahurangi*, in the 1973 Auckland–Suva race. As the race came to an end he decided that he rather enjoyed the life of a cruising wastrel and so spent most of the next decade simply cruising and racing around the world. Upon his eventual return to Auckland he stayed on the water, working on the barges that moved freight and stock around the top half of the North Island.

He also quickly resumed his love affair with fishing for snapper on his beloved Hauraki Gulf and soon earned the title 'Captain Swish' for his ability to regularly and comprehensively out-fish his mates.

Over the last 15 years, Bruce has written for most of New Zealand's top boating and fishing magazines and his information-packed articles now appear in *NZ Fishing News* and the *Outboarder*.

Bruce also regularly gives talks on how to improve one's fishing and appeared in the iconic fishing video 'Snapper Secrets' by Geoff Thomas. He still lives in Kohimarama, is married to Alison and goes fishing on their 9.2 metre Reflections Sportsfisher *Miss B Haven* 'about once or twice a week — sometimes more!'

Mike Rose is an experienced marine magazine writer, editor and photographer. His articles and photographs have appeared in magazines and publications throughout the world, including Australia, the United Kingdom and South Africa. He now runs a successful public relations business in Auckland and is the New Zealand correspondent for the Australian-based *Club Marine* Magazine.

A keen if not always successful fisherman, it was Mike who first encouraged Bruce to start sharing his knowledge by writing articles about fishing. The original arrangement was that Bruce would teach Mike how to fish and Mike would return the favour by teaching Bruce how to take good photos. The pair still argues about who got the best end of the deal . . .

How to Use This Book

Once you have chosen the area you wish to target, focus on the spots for either summer (marked with a black fish symbol —) or winter (marked with a grey fish symbol —) depending on the time of year. Then turn the page for more information on each spot, including its ideal combination of wind and tide.

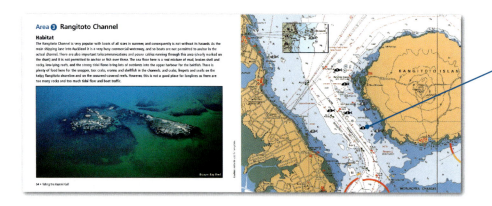

Summer Spot N° 4
This indicates the approximate position of the spot and whether it fishes best in winter or summer. More detailed information about the spot will be found on the following page.

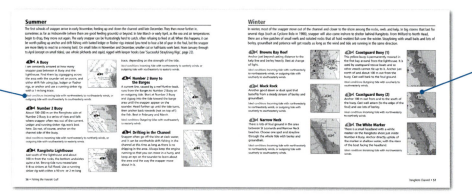

Ideal conditions
These are the best combinations of wind and tide for this spot, particularly useful if you want to get your lines and berley flowing in the same direction — or avoid rolling your guts out in a wind-against-tide sea.

Close-up Winter Spot N° 5
This positions the spot more accurately on the chart, as well as giving a brief description of the area and the best way of fishing here.

Note: Charts are provided as a guide only and must not be used for navigation.

Areas Covered in This Book

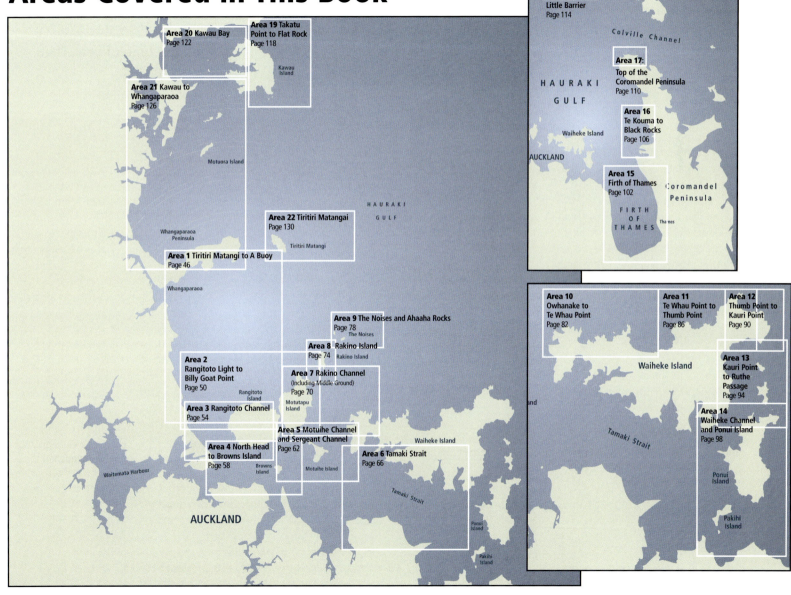

Area 20 Kawau Bay
Page 122

Area 19 Takatu
Point to Flat Rock
Page 118

Kawau Island

Area 21 Kawau to
Whangaparaoa
Page 126

Motuora Island

Whangaparaoa
Peninsula

Whangaparaoa

Area 22 Tiritiri Matangai
Page 130

HAURAKI
GULF

Tiritiri Matangi

Area 1 Tiritiri Matangi to A Buoy
Page 46

Area 9 The Noises and Ahaaha Rocks
Page 78
The Noises

Area 8 Rakino Island
Page 74
Rakino Island

Area 2
Rangitoto Light to
Billy Goat Point
Page 50

Rangitoto
Island

Area 7 Rakino Channel
(Including Middle Ground)
Page 70

Motutapu
Island

Area 3 Rangitoto Channel
Page 54

Area 5 Motuihe Channel
and Sergeant Channel
Page 62

Area 4 North Head
to Browns Island
Page 58

Browns
Island

Motuihe Island

Area 6 Tamaki Strait
Page 66

Waiheke Island

Waitemata Harbour

Tamaki Strait

AUCKLAND

Ponui
Island

Pakihi
Island

Little
Barrier
Island

Great
Barrier
Island

Area 18
Little Barrier
Page 114

Colville Channel

HAURAKI

GULF

Area 17:
Top of the
Coromandel Peninsula
Page 110

Waiheke Island

Area 16
Te Kouma to
Black Rocks
Page 106

AUCKLAND

Area 15
Firth of Thames
Page 102

Coromandel
Peninsula

FIRTH
OF
THAMES

Thames

Area 10
Owhanake to
Te Whau Point
Page 82

Area 11
Te Whau Point to
Thumb Point
Page 86

Area 12
Thumb Point to
Kauri Point
Page 90

Waiheke Island

Area 13
Kauri Point
to Ruthe
Passage
Page 94

Area 14
Waiheke Channel
and Ponui Island
Page 98

Tamaki Strait

Ponui
Island

Pakihi
Island

Understanding Snapper

To catch snapper successfully in the Hauraki Gulf takes knowledge and skill. Those people who regularly go home with fish in the bin have taken the time to understand how snapper live and feed and, just as importantly, have taken the time to understand the habitat of the snapper they are targeting.

The Hauraki Gulf is a huge, relatively shallow area, with a mainly muddy or sandy sea floor full of shellfish, crabs, shrimps and worms. It is an ideal habitat for snapper as, not only is there an abundance of food, but the shallow, sheltered waters also provide a perfect environment in which they can spawn.

Snapper usually arrive in the Gulf in schools in early October. At this stage the schools are largely male or female and will remain this way until after the fish have spawned. Pre-spawning snapper can be among the most difficult fish to catch, appearing in big schools on the sounder yet often refusing to take a bait regardless of what is offered. Suddenly, as though a switch has been thrown, they will become voracious feeders, but only on one type of bait. Then, perhaps just five minutes later, they will change again to another bait type, ignoring what was previously popular. This 'bite' usually lasts about 15–20 minutes, although it can be as brief as five minutes or as long as an hour.

At the start of the spawning season, the bite seems to occur during the first and last hours of the tide, and this changes by about an hour a week until it has gone full circle. This can be an enormously frustrating time to fish as the big schools on the sounder do not translate into big catches in the fish bin. If all else fails, try drifting through the schools using a jig, a flasher or a baited ledger rig. This might entice the fish to feed, or to lash out in aggression, and either way you may get hooked up.

Once the water temperature reaches 18°C, the snapper rise to the surface and spawn. They then become very aggressive feeders, spurred on by the greater competition for food and the need to restore lost condition. As a result, bigger baits often prove very successful.

On days of small tides or bad moon phases, snapper seem to become lazy and feed less; at these times it is necessary to target areas with strong tide runs. During such periods the Rangitoto and Motuihe channels become popular as the snapper bite harder in the faster-flowing waters.

As summer draws to a close, the need to build condition for the winter becomes more intense and the competition for food among snapper becomes greater. By February, many snapper will have moved into the harbours and up into the shallows in their search for food. They will often remain there until late April, when the food becomes harder to find and the water temperature begins to drop. Most of the snapper then leave for deeper water, allowing the harbours and shallows time to regenerate before the next summer migration.

However, not all snapper leave these sheltered waters, some preferring to stay around the rocks and reefy, kelp- and seaweed-covered shorelines where the limpets, snails, shellfish and crabs become their diet for the winter. As they are in good condition, with a high body-fat content, these resident winter snapper do not need to eat much and are provided with good protection from the winter storms by the rocks and reefs. As a result, it is necessary first to tempt them out of their protected shelter and then to entice them to eat. Berley and groundbait are essential weapons in this campaign, and small, oily baits such as half pilchards or strips of

A couple of fat winter snapper caught within sight of downtown Auckland.

mullet or bonito often prove more effective than bigger baits. These winter snapper stay in the shallows until the water starts to warm up, when they move out into the channels to join the pre-spawning snapper as they arrive and another season begins.

Remember, the only way to improve your fishing skills is to put in time on the water. Fishing is a very three-dimensional sport, where habitat, weather and time of the season all play a big part. The key to catching more snapper lies in understanding where they are and how they are feeding. Use this book, combined with your own experience, to target a spot where the wind and tide are right, and then stay there. Keep a diary of the conditions, the time the fish come on the bite, and the type and size of the baits they prefer. As your understanding of the habitat and the habits of the snapper grows, so will the size of your catches. However, please think of future generations and keep only what you can eat fresh.

Choosing the Right Equipment

How do you decide which rod and reel combination is best for you? My wife once asked me why I needed 18 different rods and reels, and I replied: 'Have you ever tried to play a round of golf with just one club?'

As you read this book, you'll realise that I'm a strong believer in the 'habitat is where it's at' strategy when it comes to targeting snapper. As long as snapper choose to live in a variety of different habitats at different depths and in different current strengths, anglers will need different combinations with which to catch them. Having said that, a couple of well-matched sets is a good starting kit for targeting snapper in the Hauraki Gulf.

When deciding which set to buy, be aware of its size, weight and balance. Unbalanced or heavy sets are not only clumsy and difficult to use, but can also lead to the development of a bad technique with the consequent loss of fish. This is particularly important with young children, who get bored and grumpy if they have to struggle with a set that is obviously too big for them.

Straylining Combinations

The best rods to use for straylining are those

Use spinning rods and reels (in Bruce's left hand) for straylining and overhead combinations (in Bruce's right hand) for deep-water fishing.

commonly referred to as spinning rods. These have larger guides that are also set further apart, and are designed to be used with fixed-spool, or 'eggbeater', reels. Ideal for casting, the larger guides are designed to allow the line to run quickly and freely from the reel to the rod tip, giving greater distance and more accuracy to the cast.

Some fixed-spool reels have a secondary drag system which can be a very useful feature when targeting big snapper in shallow water.

This combination of spinning rod and fixed-spool reel is perfect for straylining in depths up to 15 m, especially where there is little tidal run. It allows the average angler to achieve distance and accuracy from their casts without the danger of those horrible bird's-nest tangles. Another big advantage of this type of combination is that spare spools are available for most fixed-spool reels, making it very easy to change from one line weight to another if conditions change.

The drag on a fixed-spool reel is adjusted using a plastic control knob or wheel on the top. Some fixed-spool reels have a secondary drag system. There are a number of different names for this, depending on the brand. The one I use is a Penn Liveliner. This secondary system can be a very useful feature when targeting big snapper in shallow water as it allows the fish to 'test' the bait without feeling any pressure from the line. When using reels with this feature, set the main drag properly and then set the secondary drag so that it is just tight enough to stop the current dragging away the bait. Big fish (which have reached their size by being very cautious) often run only a short distance with the bait held loosely in their mouth. Allow the fish to run and then stop before you turn off the secondary drag. Strike only when the fish moves off for the second time.

Be sure children have the right-sized gear as they will probably get grumpy and bored if they are forced to use a set that is obviously too big for them.

Casting Tips

Take the line in one finger and pull it back and up to the reel seat on the rod. This will stop the line from falling off the face of the reel, giving you more control at the time of release. If you are having difficulty mastering the art of casting, take your rig into a large, clear area such as a sports field and put down a target. Once you can hit this target regularly, move further back and try again. Try in tail, head and cross winds to develop the skills that allow you to place a bait exactly where you want it.

Deep-water Combinations

Rods and reels designed for deeper water are often called overhead rods or reels as they are fished with the rod guides and the reel on top of the rod. Because the line lies along the top of the rod, overhead rods generally have a lot more guides than spinning rods — these keep the line off the rod when it is loaded up or bent downwards when fighting a fish.

In deeper water and channels where the tidal run is strong, a correctly rigged overhead reel will recover line directly on to the reel drum with little or no line twist. In the same conditions, the line often becomes very twisted (and therefore weakened) on a fixed-spool reel because it uses rotary action to recover the line. Some of the better overhead reels also feature an excellent piece of equipment called a level wind. This sits over the front of the reel and moves back and forth as line is recovered, thereby ensuring an even distribution across the whole width of the reel.

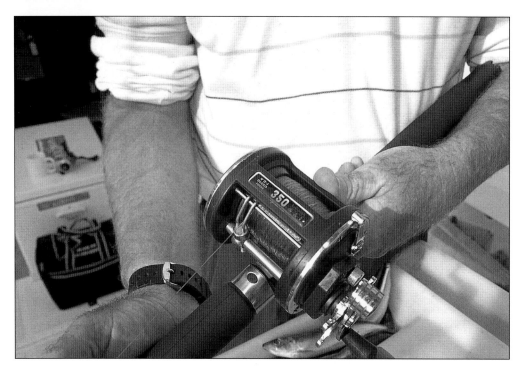

Some of the better overhead reels also feature an excellent piece of equipment called a level wind which ensures an even distribution across the whole width of the reel.

On an overhead reel, drag is usually set using a spoked metal wheel on the side. However, some reels do feature an easy-to-set lever drag system for even better control.

Understanding Rods

Today's rods are very different from the short, solid fibreglass 'stump pullers' of old, and most now feature advanced composite construction. Ask for those models that feature a one-piece extruded section (such as the Jarvis Walker Whitetail range) rather than an insert at the tip. Both types may look the same, with a clear, white or different coloured section at the top, but the single-extrusion rods last longer and retain their powerful lifting action and sensitive tip better. If in doubt, check with the experts at your local tackle shop.

Lightweight carbon-fibre rods are becoming increasingly popular, but note that they must be treated with lots of care as they are very easy to damage. Sharp contact (such as knocking against a rocket launcher during a vigorous strike) will appear to leave only a small scratch yet may

Rods with larger guides, set further apart (right), are better for use with spinning reels when straylining.

or try to use the rod to break it off. You will not only crush the nylon onto the spool, but you will also risk breaking the rod. Instead, pull off enough line to allow you to lay the rod away somewhere safe, then pull on the line with your hand. Regardless of whether the line breaks off or is retrieved intact, it will have been stretched and therefore weakened (often by more than 50 per cent), so it should always be replaced. Cut the line in your hand and then pull the rest on board and dump it somewhere safe.

It also pays to check the line regularly as it can easily be damaged by rubbing against or over shell, rocks or kelp. Again, damaged line should always be replaced as soon as possible. If line is continually being damaged, even when you are fishing over clean ground, check for cracks in the rod guides. Do this by running a nylon stocking through the guides — if the nylon snags, the guides need to be replaced.

Maintenance of Equipment

After every fishing trip, thoroughly wash all rods and reels, even those that have just sat in the rocket launcher or rod holders — salt spray is just as corrosive as the seawater itself. Do not, however, blast your gear with a powerful hose as this only drives the salt particles deeper in. Instead, gently hose away the worst of the salt and then use a soft nylon brush and warm, soapy, fresh water. Finally, starting at the rod tip and working down, thoroughly rinse with fresh water. Be sure to loosen the drag to prevent the drag washers from compressing and sticking.

easily create a weak spot that will break under load. And, as you know, Murphy's Law says it will break while you are battling the biggest fish you have ever seen . . .

Setting the Drag

Getting the drag right is critical, regardless of whether you are using an overhead or a fixed-spool reel. Ensure that the line can be pulled from the reel by hand; if you cannot do so, it will break under the load of a big fish. If in doubt, ask the team at your local tackle shop for help.

Looking after the Line

The line on your reel is the only thing between you and the fish, and if it is damaged, stretched, crushed or otherwise compromised it stands a good chance of breaking, probably on a very good fish. Most fishing line is made of nylon and it is helpful to think of it as not dissimilar to a plastic bag. If you keep pulling on a plastic bag it will get thinner and thinner until it eventually breaks; nylon fishing line is exactly the same. Therefore, if you get stuck in the foul, do not wind furiously on the reel

All About Bait

Having good-quality bait and presenting it properly are two of the most important factors in a successful day's fishing.

Many anglers defrost frozen baits in a bucket of water, but while this does give instant bait it also causes the flesh cells to break down quickly. This makes the bait mushy, hard to rig properly and unlikely to stay on the hooks. Instead, it is far better to take enough bait for the first two hours' fishing out of the freezer the night before, wrap it up tightly in a section of newspaper, and then leave it so that it defrosts slowly and in a controlled fashion. The next morning, the bait will look fresh and firm and be ready to use. In winter, bigger, thicker-fleshed baits such as whole bonito (skipjack tuna), mullet or kahawai will take longer to defrost and so should be taken out of the freezer and wrapped in newspaper in the late afternoon or early evening of the previous day. The first couple of centimetres of a berley bomb treated in the same way will be soft, and so will

Piper, which are one of my favourite fresh baits, tend to hang a little way back from the boat.

disperse instantly to create an attractive berley trail the moment it hits the water.

However, when it comes to bait there is no doubt that fresh is best. Catching your own is also a great way to keep both kids and adults amused while at the same time providing free bait.

Attracting baitfish to the boat is just another good reason for using berley, and a

berley trail will soon be full of useful little fish just waiting to be turned into bait. I find a weighted flasher rig is the easiest way to catch baitfish, although a light line with a tiny piece of bait (small pieces of squid tentacles stay on best) will also do the trick.

Koheru (often called yellowtail), piper and slimy mackerel all make excellent fresh bait and can usually be found throughout

the Hauraki Gulf. However, sprats, which are also very common, do not work anywhere near as well. I find that sprats are best scaled and then butterflied, or chopped into small pieces for groundbait (see 'Berley and Groundbait', page 32). Piper, which are one of my favourite fresh baits, tend to hang a little way back from the boat. Although there are a number of ways to catch them, I find that a light line with a float, cast 3–4 m astern, gets the best results.

Netting for Bait

When selecting a bait net, I always choose one that has been designed specifically to target piper as these have a smaller mesh size than other general bait nets. (Piper can escape through a bait net, but a piper net will also catch baitfish.)

As baitfish scare easily and swim fast, your net must be ready to go before you begin. Set up the net in a fish bin or something similar so that it will flow straight out without tangles. Do this by gently flaking (folding) the net into the bin, working from side to side and using the whole width of the bin. Ideally, two people — one on the float line and one on the lead line — should flake the net into the bin so that the floats are at one end and the lead line is on the other.

Choose a nice sheltered bay and then use berley to attract the baitfish into the shallows. Bread is good for this, although if it is simply thrown onto the water it will attract seagulls, which will scare away the fish. Instead, pre-soak and mush the bread

Always ensure the barb of the hook is completely clear of the bait, regardless of whether you are using a single hook or keeper-hooked pilchard (above) or a butterflied bait for big snapper (below).

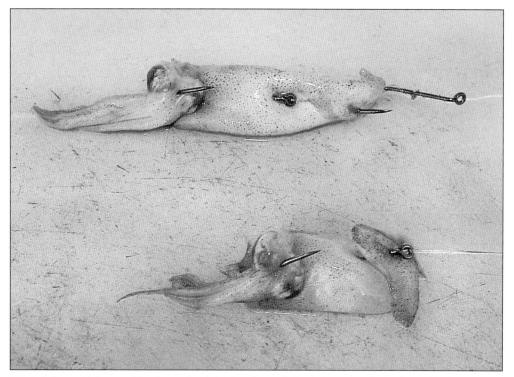

Whole baby squid rigged with a keeper hook (top) and a single hook. Note that the hooks and barbs are well exposed and set through the top of the tentacles.

onshore wades out until he or she is knee-deep in water, while the rower moves away until a third of the net is out. Next, the rower moves parallel to the beach until another third is out, and then he or she heads back to the shore.

Retrieving the Net
Squatting down (to keep the lead line hard on the bottom so that no baitfish can escape under the net), pull in both ends of the net at the same time, piling it behind you as you do so. Be sure to pull the net in slowly to prevent it from lifting off the bottom, allowing the fish to escape.

Freezing your Bait
If you plan on freezing freshly caught bait for later use it is important that you freeze the fish individually rather than in a big heap. Cover a flat board or scone tray with cling film and then lay the baitfish out on this, making sure the fish are straight and not touching one another. Cover them with cling film and freeze them on the board. Once the fish are frozen, they can be removed from the cling film and bagged up together ready for use.

Bait Presentation
Bait presentation is, I believe, the single most important factor in hooking snapper. On one occasion when the fishing was hot, I was fishing in a small boat with two mates. Yet while I had caught my limit, these two had not had a single bite between them and were getting decidedly grumpy. When I checked their baits, I found

up so that it sinks quickly.

Be patient and watch the water surface until you see the baitfish feeding on the berley. Once they start feeding, it is vital to run the net around them as quickly as possible. Using a dinghy is best, although hand hauling can be just as effective.

Hand Hauling
First, gather up half the net and then walk out into the bay, a little way from the feeding school, towing the rest of the net behind you. Once the other end of the net (on the beach) is in knee-deep water, slowly let the net pull out of your hands as you go around the baitfish. (Do not try to drag the net off the beach, as this is too slow and too difficult.)

Using a Dinghy
Set the fish bin at the stern of the boat so that the net can run out freely. The person

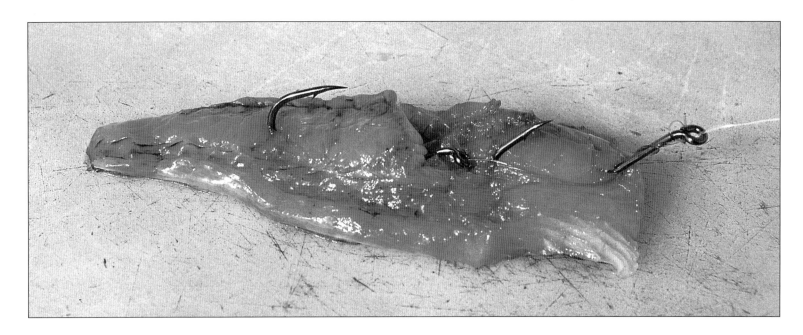

that they were bent — in other words, lying sideways in the current in a most unnatural fashion. I re-rigged them properly, and as soon as the baits hit the bottom they hooked fish. Luck had nothing to do with it: it was all in the presentation.

Baits must be presented naturally. This is never more true than when the snapper are particularly fussy, as they tend to be during the pre-spawning period in late spring/early summer and, particularly, during the winter.

Exposing the Barb

A lot of anglers seem to think snapper can see their hooks and therefore go to great lengths to hide them, burying the barbs in their bait. This is wrong! The exact opposite is actually the case: exposed barbs are

A twin-hook strip bait using big (7/0 or bigger) hooks ensures the barbs are well clear. Big hooks also mean any small fish are only lip-hooked and so easier to release unharmed.

absolutely essential to ensure a good hook-up rate. If you are constantly dropping the fish after a couple of winds of the reel, check whether the barb is well clear of the bait; if it is buried, it will simply slide out of the hard, strong interior of the snapper's mouth. A properly exposed barb will hook into the jaw of the fish when pulled up, resulting in a far better catch rate. Try running a finger over the bait — if the hook doesn't catch you, it certainly won't catch a snapper.

Hook Size

Hook size is also critical, for two reasons:

small hooks are hard to rig so that the barb is exposed; and small hooks also tend to gut-hook small fish that should be released unharmed (see 'Fish Handling and Conservation', page 138).

Big hooks (I always use 7/0s) are easy to rig so that the barbs are well clear of the bait. They are also too big for small fish to swallow (lip-hooked undersized snapper have a far better chance of survival when released than ones that have been gut-hooked). Large hooks are also easier to remove without stressing fish that are to be released.

Successful Straylining Rigs

Snapper can be very bait-shy, and at such times smaller half- or strip baits will prove more successful than whole pilchards or squid. If you use a half-bait, cut the baitfish through the gut cavity so that the juices leach out like a miniature berley trail.

Pilchard Rigs

These are also suitable for piper, sprats and other baitfish. Always rig pilchards (which are a pretty soft bait) through the head so that they can be cast without being damaged.

Single-hook Rig

Bring the hook up through the gill plate and right through the top of the skull. After pulling the hook well clear of the fish, push it straight down again (with the barb facing away from the head) until it is stopped by the curve of the shank. Then push the shank of the hook forward so the barb travels under and up the opposite side of the backbone until the barb is well clear of the bait.

Use this rig for picky pre- and post-spawning snapper, and particularly for winter fish.

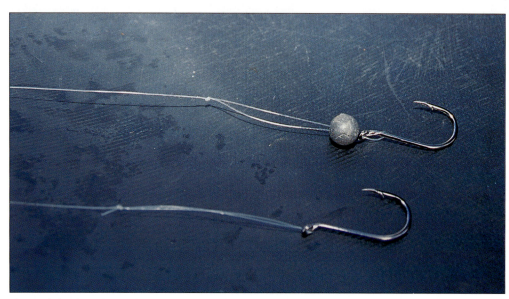

The single-hook rig is good for picky pre- and post-spawning snapper and for winter fishing.

Two-hook Keeper Rig

A keeper-hook rig consists of one hook (the main hook) tied directly onto the end of the line (or trace), with the other hook (the keeper hook) able to slide freely. Both hooks should be the same size (7/0 or bigger). Lay the pilchard on its side and thread the main hook directly through the middle of the fish. Then hold the pilchard the right way up and facing away from you, and push the hook straight down again (with the barb facing away from the head) until it is stopped by the curve of the shank. Then push the shank of the hook forward so the barb travels under

A keeper-hook rig consists of one hook tied directly onto the end of the line, with the other hook able to slide freely. Use this rig for deep-water and channel fishing, and for summer straylining.

Squid Rigs

Snapper of all sizes just love squid tentacles and will often rip them off and then leave the rest of the bait alone. Therefore the essence of a good squid rig is to place the head/tentacles over the barb of the hook.

Single-hook Rig

Baby squid are an ideal bait for shy snapper and are easily rigged on a single hook. Simply fold the squid in half, push the hook through the folded section at the top of the fold and then slide this up the shank. Next, push the barb right through the bait just above the base of the mantle. Now bring the head/tentacles up so you can then push the barb of the hook through the middle of the head (not through the squid's eyes).

Use this rig for picky pre- and post-spawning snapper, and particularly for winter fish.

Whole-squid Keeper Rig

Do the same as above with the bottom hook but do not fold the squid in half. Then slide the keeper hook down so the eye is level with the top of the squid, wind the line three times around the shank, push the hook in one side of the squid and out the other and repeat. Be sure both barbs are clearly exposed.

Use this rig for deep-water and channel fishing, and for summer straylining.

and up the opposite side of the backbone until the barb is well clear of the bait. Next, pull the line tight and slide the keeper hook down so that the barb is parallel with the middle of the head. Wind the line around the shank of the hook at least three times and pull tight to take up the slack. This will prevent the bait from bending. Finally, push the keeper hook between the gill plates until the barb is exposed above the skull. Use this rig for deep-water and channel fishing, and for summer straylining.

Above: Drift fishing with a baited flasher rig is a quick and easy way to check whether marks on the sounder are snapper or schools of baitfish.

Right: On a flasher or ledger rig, sinkers on a light trace will break free if snagged.

Monster Bait Rig

This is very similar to the two-hook keeper rig but on a grand scale. Use half a kahawai, mullet or bonito head. Traces should be about 0.5–1 m long with at least 24 kg breaking strain. Use two 9/0 or 10/0 hooks. Instead of positioning the keeper hook through the middle of the head, place it further forward so that it is well exposed in front of the eyes. Use this rig for targeting deeper-water or straylined large and extra-large snapper.

Baiting Pilchard
Pilchard

Step ❶
Bring the hook up through the gill plate and right through the top of the skull.

Squid

Step ❶
Push the hook through the 'bottom' of the squid near the head and then slide this up the shank.

and Squid

Step ❷
After pulling the hook well clear of the fish, push it straight down again (with the barb facing away from the head) until it is stopped by the curve of the shank.

Step ❸
Push the shank of the hook forward so the barb travels under and up the opposite side of the backbone.

Step ❹
Ensure the barb is well clear of the bait. Use this rig for picky pre-and post-spawning or shy winter snapper.

Step ❷
Push the barb right through the bait again just above the base of the mantle and then bring the head/tentacles up so you can then push the barb of the hook through the middle of the head (not through the squid's eyes).

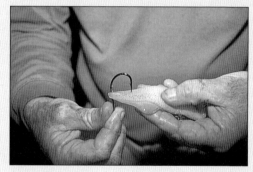

Step ❸
Slide the keeper hook down so the eye is level with the top of the squid, wind the line three times around the shank and push the hook in one side of the squid and out the other and repeat.

Step ❹
Be sure both barbs are clearly exposed. Use this rig for deep water and channel fishing and for summer straylining.

Straylining

Straylining is the most exciting method of fishing as the angler is connected directly to the bait and can feel every little bit of action from the fish, whether it is a young, brash snapper charging in at speed or a wily old moocher taking a tentative taste before swallowing. In shallower water, the fish fight more fiercely and there is always something to do. For me, straylining is fishing.

When I first started fishing several decades ago, most anglers anchoring their boat in the channels tied on big hunks of lead to get their baits down, and used relatively small pieces of bait and short, stumpy rods. Once the bait had been dropped, there was little to do except wait for the rod to start to bend. The rod was stuck in the rod holder and left — there was little point in trying to feel a bite over the weight of the lead and little point in trying to strike, for by the time the movement of the rod being struck reached the bait, the snapper was on its way to Peru! It was a

Straylining is most effective during the winter months, and in spring and autumn when the resident snapper are still living in among the rocks and reefs.

pretty passive sort of fishing, and a lot of passengers got very bored (and often quite seasick) as they rolled around in the channel waiting for a school of snapper to pass by.

In contrast, straylining is a very active form of fishing that really is fun for the whole family. A berley trail has to be set and then maintained, groundbait has to be added constantly, baits need to be checked and replaced, and, hopefully, fish are fought and landed. So what exactly is straylining? Straylining is basically fishing with relatively light line in relatively shallow water, using the absolute minimum weight to get the bait down to the waiting fish. The usual straylining rig is a very simple affair: a single hook tied directly to the end of the line, with either no sinker at all or a very small sinker that slides freely just above the hook.

To strayline successfully you will need the right equipment (see 'Choosing the Right Equipment', page 14). This consists of a longish, 'whippy' rod suitable for casting and an eggbeater style of reel. You need the lightest line possible — 6–8 kg breaking strain is good, and definitely no more than 10 kg (anything heavier is too difficult to cast and will spook the snapper) — and reasonably large hooks (7/0) to protect the smaller fish (see 'Fish Handling and Conservation', page 138).

Straylining is most effective during the winter months, and in spring and autumn when the resident snapper are still living in among the rocks and reefs. It can also be successful in summer, but usually a little further out over sandy or muddy bottoms where there is relatively little

If the fish is well hooked and only of moderate size, you can lift it into the boat by hand. Never bring it in using the rod.

tidal flow. Straylining is also particularly effective at dawn or dusk, when the combination of lightweight tackle and the change of light seems to encourage otherwise shy fish to feed.

There are a number of excellent straylining spots covered in this book and you will soon learn to find your own. Do this by remembering the old adage: 'habitat is where it's at'. Look for rocky structures and reefs around headlands or along kelpy shorelines, especially those that have a gut or channel running through them. Ensure that the tide and wind are running in the same direction and that they will hold the boat so that the stern faces the target area. The current must be running from the boat on to the reef or rocks and ideally through any channels. Work out where you want your baits to land (generally just before the kelpy edge of the structure so that they are over a clean bottom and not actually on the reef) and then anchor far enough away so that you cast to this area.

Straylining is by nature a relatively shallow-water style of fishing (I usually anchor in just 4–12 m) and it is therefore very important not to frighten away the fish.

quietly as possible, and then turn off the sounder and the stereo. If you are fishing with other boats, try to get them to arrive and position themselves at the same time. I have often been in a situation where I have been settled in and catching fish when another boat has come along to see how I am doing. Even when they have been very considerate and always stayed well forward and well away from my baits, the fishing has instantly died and not resumed until at least half an hour after they have either anchored or moved off.

Once the boat has been positioned correctly, throw a couple of different baits in different directions, just to test the water,

Snapper are a shy fish and will not hang around and feed if they are aware there are people or boats about. Straylining is therefore a lot like hunting in that it is necessary to sneak up on the fish and then try to make as little noise as possible.

Anchor at the end of your casting range and use berley and groundbait to entice the fish out to your baits. Always approach a likely spot as slowly as possible (this is good seamanship, too, as there could be rocks about), lower the anchor as gently and

Run the line over your finger so you feel even the smallest of bites.

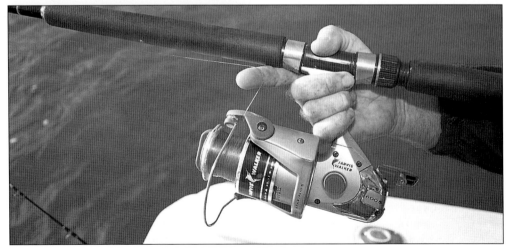

while you prepare the berley and groundbait. While it is unlikely that these first few baits will catch fish, you never know. These early baits will hopefully show whether you have the right amount of weight on and possibly even which bait and which area is going to fish the best.

The next task is to get the berley trail going (see 'Berley and Groundbait', page 32) and to throw out some groundbait to entice the snapper. Be sure to throw the groundbait in as wide an arc as possible and as far away as possible (you'll never attract snapper to feed directly under the boat in shallow water — they are far too shy). Next, set a pattern of baits in a semi-circle from the transom by casting out to each side as well as directly astern. Be sure to vary the distance of your casts as you will often initially catch fish reasonably close to the boat and then, as the berley starts to spread, the bigger fish will be drawn out from the rocks and kelp.

Always use a range of baits as snapper will sometimes take one bait for an hour or so and then switch to another. If your fishing partner is catching all the fish and you are not even getting a bite, it may pay to check what bait he or she is using and switch to that. It is also important to check and replace baits regularly as any that have been nibbled at and dislodged from the hook are much less likely to attract a fish than properly rigged, fresh ones. My favourite baits for straylining are pilchards and squid or, even better, fresh baits such as a piper or koheru that have been caught in the berley trail.

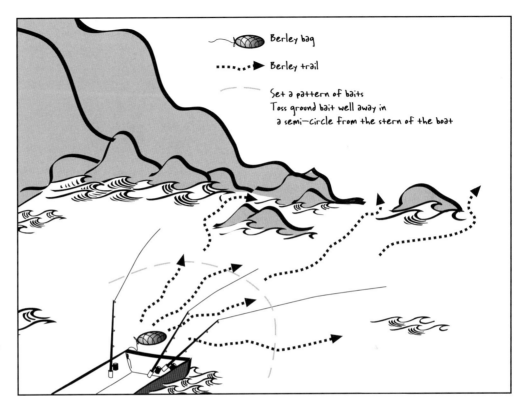

Berley bag

Berley trail

Set a pattern of baits
Toss ground bait well away in
a semi-circle from the stern of the boat

Depending on how many other anglers are on board, I always fish with at least two rods, using a different type of bait on each. As in the setting of a pattern of baits, this is what I call 'covering the bases', and it is a very important part of any fishing, especially straylining. Fishing is not an exact science, for we cannot see what is under the water but can only use our experience and cunning to try to find and then catch our quarry. Covering the bases in as many ways as possible greatly enhances our chances of getting it right, as well as helping us learn

about what works and what does not and at what stages of the tide and season. Such local knowledge and experience is what creates good anglers.

When not holding the rod, place it as low as possible in the boat rather than in the rod holder, and ensure that one of the guides is firmly up against the transom or some other fixed part of the boat (there's nothing worse than watching a big fish take your bait, only to see it take your rod as well!). Always try to hold at least one rod in your hand so you can feel any interest from the fish down

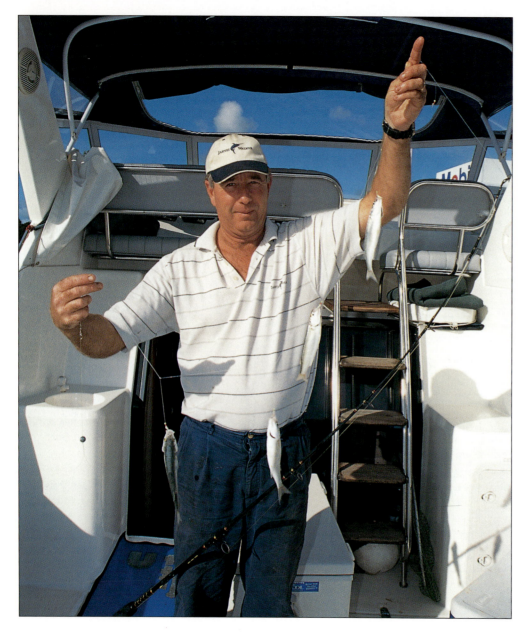

below. Pre-spawning snapper and wily old moochers both tend to pick up baits and either crush them in their mouths or simply hold them for a few moments, and it's easy to mistake these 'tap, taps' for the darting runs of small snapper. Ensure that the tip of the rod you are holding is pointing at the same angle to the water as the line and run the line over your finger. This enables you to feel even the smallest of bites and to raise the rod tip slowly to feel whether the snapper still has the bait in its mouth. When you feel the weight, strike hard at the fish — you will often be surprised at the size of the fish you catch from these small touches.

Once the fish is hooked, be sure to keep the rod tip up and let the fish run if it wants to. One of the great advantages of straylining is that even quite small fish fight well above their weight in shallow water, and you will enjoy some great battles with 1–2-kg snapper on a whippy rod.

Remember to let the rod do the work: the reel is there to retrieve line won back by the rod, not to winch the fish in. Using as smooth an action as possible, lift the rod and then wind in as the rod is slowly lowered. Keep a constant bend in the rod, do not drop it below a 45-degree angle, and always ensure the line is tight — if there is any slack, the snapper has a good chance of throwing the hook and escaping. Always fight fish in this way, regardless of their size. Lowering the rod and simply winching in

A baited flasher rig will often catch baitfish which, when butterflied, are ideal for targeting big snapper by straylining into the reefy shoreline on dusk.

Once the fish is hooked, be sure to keep the rod tip up and let the fish run if it wants to.

good chance you'll lose it) or to scoop the net under the fish (you'll probably spook it, and it will then do another run and possibly get away).

If the fish is well hooked and only of moderate size, you can lift it into the boat by hand. Never bring it in using the rod, or you will risk damaging the rod tip and create chaos on board as you try to deal with a stroppy fish with a big rod hanging off it! Instead, stop winding once the fish hits the surface, carefully lay down the rod and quickly lift the fish on board. Decide whether you are going to keep the fish or return it to the sea, and then either kill it quickly using the iki method or release it safely (see 'Fish Handling and Conservation', page 138).

smaller fish only fosters bad habits, which will then be found out when a bigger opponent comes along. Use smaller fish for practice, perfecting your technique so you are ready for that fish of a lifetime when it comes along.

If the fish is a reasonably sized one or you are concerned that the hook is not well set, use a landing net to bring it on board. Do not use a gaff as there is the chance that the point will slide off the snapper's large scales. Place the net in the water and lead the fish to it by slowly walking backwards. Do not try to swing the fish into the net (there's a

Ensure that the tip of the rod is pointing at the same angle to the water as the line.

Berley and Groundbait

Berley

To understand how berley works, imagine coming home at night and opening the front door after someone has been cooking a roast dinner. The smell instantly makes you think 'food' and you start to feel hungry. You then move towards the source of the food, anxious to see if it looks and tastes as good as it smells . . .

Berley works on fish in exactly the same way. They smell the fine mist as it moves down along the tide line, think 'Yum!' and go looking for dinner. The key to successful berleying is to ensure a constant, non-stop flow at the right depth (remember: you cannot have too much berley in the water). In shallow water (less than 10 m) when the current is not strong, tie the berley bag from the transom so that it floats on the surface. Be sure to place it in an accessible place so

Berley is often placed in onion bags or something similar to allow for easy dispersal. However, when shaken regularly, the mesh of these bags can become clogged with larger pieces of berley, dramatically reducing the flow. You can overcome this problem by making a number of cuts down the sides and along the bottom of the bag.

that it is easy to 'work' (in other words, shake vigorously) from time to time. This will ensure that a steady stream of berley makes its way down to the sea floor (in gentle currents, it travels as little as 30 m behind the boat, but in stronger flows it can go up to a mile and a half).

Snapper, which always face into a current and feed across it, will quickly pick up the scent of the berley and work their way towards you. The longer the berley trail is maintained, the further this scent will spread and the more fish will be attracted from a very wide area.

In deeper water and in stronger currents, it will be necessary to weigh the berley bag down to ensure the berley reaches the bottom relatively close to the back of the boat. Use a couple of dive weights or something similar. It is important that the berley bag is set about 1 m off the bottom, especially if it is tied to the anchor warp (see illustration opposite, below): this allows the movement of the boat literally to 'shake' the bag, ensuring a constant flow. Bags set on the chain itself or close to the anchor will lie on the bottom and move very little, giving a very poor, ineffective berley flow.

Make a number of cuts in the bag to improve the berley flow.

When fishing deep (20 m or more) reefs, I like to anchor at slack water and use two berley bags: one down the anchor warp and the other on the surface. This is really cunning stuff. The surface berley works well in slack water and early in the tide, and then starts to disperse over a very wide area, leaving the bottom bag to do all the work. At full flood, while the bottom bag is holding the fish close to the boat, the well-dispersed top berley bag starts to attract baitfish, kahawai and, if there are any around, kingfish!

It is also a good idea to use at least 1 m of spare line to tie the berley bag to the anchor warp. This saves you losing your anchor line if a shark decides to take off with the berley bag.

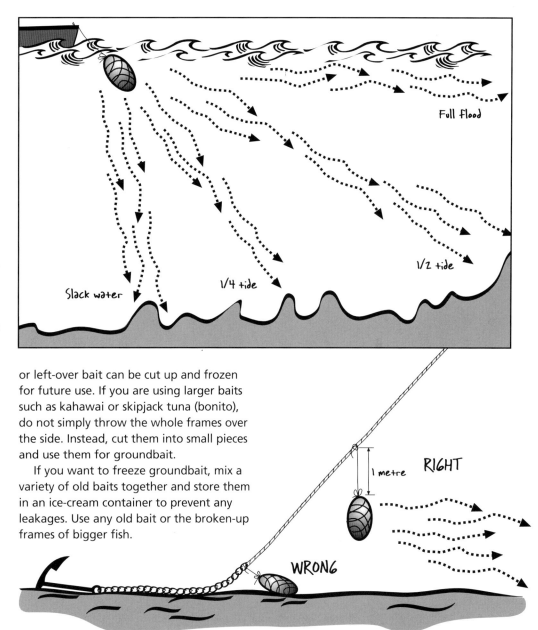

Full flood

1/2 tide

1/4 tide

Slack water

1 metre

RIGHT

WRONG

What is Berley?

Berley consists of minced-up fish frames, shellfish and pieces of fish, all usually combined with fish oil. It is available commercially from most bait outlets and there is often a choice of different types, including pilchard berley and mussel berley. Most commercial berleys now come with their own mesh bags ready for use. However, you will need to provide your own line to secure the bag to the boat or anchor warp.

Berley can also be made at home, and those who do so all seem to have at least one secret ingredient. However, any oily fish or old frames well minced up will do the trick.

Groundbait

Also known as chumming or cubing, groundbaiting involves cutting up small pieces of bait and throwing them into the tide behind the boat. Groundbaiting complements berleying, as while berley attracts the fish, it is often the groundbait that brings them on to the bite. In order to work effectively, pieces of groundbait should not be too large (or you will simply end up feeding the fish) and also need be distributed fairly regularly — about a handful every 10 minutes or so.

The best groundbait is often old bait cut into small pieces. It can be made as you go, or left-over bait can be cut up and frozen for future use. If you are using larger baits such as kahawai or skipjack tuna (bonito), do not simply throw the whole frames over the side. Instead, cut them into small pieces and use them for groundbait.

If you want to freeze groundbait, mix a variety of old baits together and store them in an ice-cream container to prevent any leakages. Use any old bait or the broken-up frames of bigger fish.

Deep-water Fishing

Successful fishing on deep-water reef structures requires considerable planning and discipline, and so it pays to make a game plan and then stick to it.

Aim to arrive at the reef at slack water and try to work out which way the boat will lie to the wind and tide. Don't just anchor at the first signs of fish. Instead, spend time using your sounder to have a good look right around the whole area. Slowly move down the reef with the sounder set on maximum zoom until you reach its end, then criss-cross back and forth, building up a picture of how big the reef is and where the best structure lies.

If you have a plotter on board, use it in conjunction with the sounder to enter an event mark at each end of the reef, at the high points and where there are the biggest concentrations of fish (see 'Sounders and Plotters', page 38). Then note the tide and wind directions, and anchor so that you are fishing back on to the reef and not off it. A quick and easy way to ensure that the fish marks are not just baitfish is to use a large-hook flasher rig. Baitfish will not generally hook up on a 7/0 baited flasher.

Although many people only use berley

Deep water is best fished with an overhead reel, ideally one with a level wind that spreads the line back on the reel evenly during the retrieve.

when straylining in shallow water, I find it works really well in deep water, too. In fact, I use not one but two berley bags: one a metre or so above the anchor chain and the other on the surface. In slack water, the trail from the surface berley bag sinks slowly. Then, as the tide picks up, it takes the berley some distance behind the boat and right over the reef (see 'Berley and Groundbait',

page 32). As soon as the anchor is safely set, throw over a handful of groundbait and continue to do this every 10–15 minutes until you stop fishing. Remember that a constant trail of berley and groundbait will bring the fish to you.

When the tide is slack or just on the turn, an unweighted bait will slowly and naturally sink to the bottom, like a dead baitfish. This

Surprisingly big snapper can easily be handled with a main line of just 8–10 kg breaking strain and the hook-up rate is always better than with heavier line.

will attract pan-size and larger snapper, which will rise up out of the kelp to take the bait. In contrast, a weighted bait will be at the mercy of small reef fish as soon as it gets to the bottom. As the tide starts to run, add only enough weight to get the baits just to the bottom. The key is to let the line down slowly so that it ends up well astern of the boat. This stops a 'belly' forming in the line between the sinker and the rod tip and allows you to stay in better contact with the bait. A belly in the line makes it much harder to feel any bites and also means that your line will not be at a 45-degree angle to the boat. This makes it much harder to detect bites or strike the fish effectively and will result in greatly decreased hook-up rates. Deep water is best fished with an overhead reel (I use a Penn 320GTI), ideally one with a level wind that spreads the line back on the reel evenly during the retrieve.

Surprisingly big snapper can easily be handled with a main line of just 8–10 kg breaking strain and the hook-up rate is always better than with heavier line. Remember, it is the lifting power of the rod that tires the fish, not the strength of the line. As with all types of fishing, it is critical to match a balanced rod and reel with good line of the correct weight (see 'Choosing the Right Equipment', page 14). For average-size snapper (up to 10 kg), a 15-kg trace is adequate, but for larger fish you will need a trace of 30 kg.

To help control the bait and stop it tangling with the mainline on the way down (as it often does with a running sinker rig), slide the sinkers onto the trace. As well as preventing tangles, this also keeps the weight where it should be — right down on the bait.

I usually use a keeper rig with 7/0 or 8/0 hooks and whole pilchards, squid or strip baits (see 'Successful Straylining Rigs', page 22) as this allows me to keep in touch with my bait. In strong currents I can also use this rig to 'walk' my bait back across the reef, by lifting the rod

Above: When targeting an outsize snapper with exceptionally large bait, rig up to at least a 24-kg trace.

Right: A quick and easy way to ensure that the fish marks are not just baitfish is to use a large-hook flasher rig.

tip and slowly letting out more line as the bait is gradually taken back by the current.

When targeting an outsize snapper with exceptionally large bait, I change to a running sinker rig on what I call a lazy line. Rig up a monster bait (see 'Successful Straylining Rigs', page 22) to at least a 24-kg trace and slowly let the sinker down while the bait remains held in your hand. Once the sinker hits the bottom, gently toss the bait well astern so that it drifts back down way behind the boat. Then put on the clicker with just enough drag to stop the line from over-running when the bait is taken.

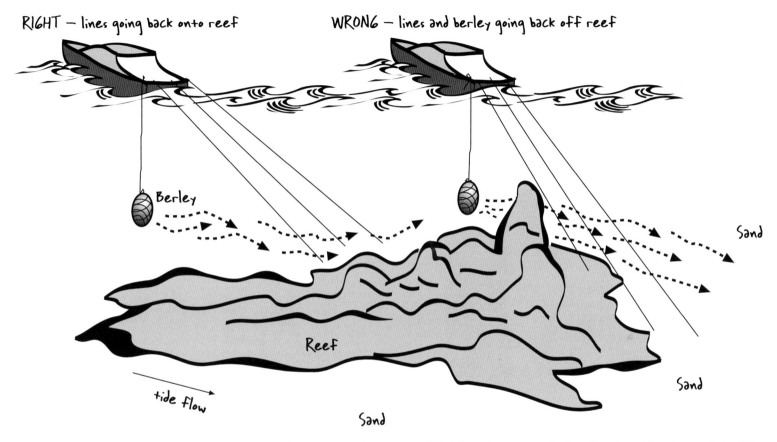

RIGHT — lines going back onto reef

WRONG — lines and berley going back off reef

Berley

Sand

Reef

tide flow

Sand

Sand

When the outsize snapper takes the bait, let it run until it slows or stops. Be patient! Hold the rod at the same angle as that of the line entering the water, lean forward and wait for the next run. When it comes, strike hard and fast and keep the rod tip high. Do not drop the rod tip. Keeping a bend in the rod at all times, start winding as you lower the rod. It is vital that you keep a constant, smooth action on the fish. If the fish runs, your drag setting will let the line go but you must keep the rod tip high when you are losing line. Keeping the rod tip high at all times allows the action of the rod to raise the head of the fish, confusing it and tiring it. A rod held naturally will not stop a fish from getting into the rocks, breaking the line and escaping.

Once the fish has tired and is coming up to the boat, ensure that you have the landing net in the water before the fish sees the boat. This stops the fish from being spooked and taking off again. Lead the fish into the net, don't chase it. A heartbreaking number of big fish are lost at the boat as a result of bad netting or gaffing. Personally I do not like to gaff snapper as it often damages them — and there are too many things that can go wrong in a lurching boat. I also prefer to release big snapper as they are the best breeding stock — and in any case these old fish are pretty tough to eat.

Sounders and Plotters

Modern marine electronics are great tools for helping us find fish, return to successful spots and enhance our understanding of the invisible world below the surface.

Understanding Sounders

Sounders — variously known as echo sounders, depth sounders, recorders, fish finders and even sonars — are basically devices that send a beam of sound down through the water layers to the sea bottom and then measure the echo of the beam when it returns. They consist of a transmitter, a receiver, a transducer and a time-measuring and indication device (such as a screen).

One of the most important parts of a sounder is the transducer. This is the bit that sits either on the transom or somewhere along the hull bottom, and that both sends and receives the signal. Transducers tend to operate at either high or low frequency, although more sophisticated models offer both. High-frequency (generally around 200 kHz) transducers use a narrower beam and have a shorter range (in other words, they work best in shallower water). In their preferred range, they offer better resolution than low-frequency models and are often

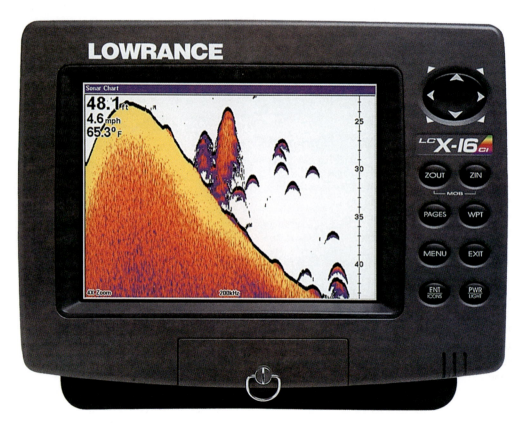

The mass of red and blue near the top of the pinnacle is typical baitfish sign, while the solid cone shapes are large individual fish.

quite a bit smaller than the latter. Low-frequency transducers (usually about 50 kHz) use a wider beam, have a longer range and are bigger in size. They work better in deep water but give a poorer-resolution picture.

For most areas of the Hauraki Gulf, which is basically shallow and rarely exceeds a depth of 50 m, a high-frequency transducer is all that is needed. However, be aware that some of the cheaper models available have been designed to work in fresh water and use a quite wide cone (or beam angle), and therefore will not provide as detailed a picture as you may wish.

Getting the Best out of a Sounder

Modern technology has made today's sounders relatively easy to use: simply turn them on and look at the sea floor below — it's like magic! However, there are a few tricks that will help you interpret better what you see on the screen — and, therefore, hopefully help you catch more fish.

The Effects of Boat Speed and Movement

The first thing to be aware of is the effect of boat speed and the way the bottom appears on the screen. It is important to remember that the faster the boat travels, the more of the bottom appears in a given slice of the screen. If you've ever been travelling along, seen a sharp drop-off on the screen, slowed down and circled back, and then not been able to find it, you'll know what I mean. The drop-off appeared steep because the sounder had to display both the top and bottom of the peak in a very small time frame; when you mooched over it again

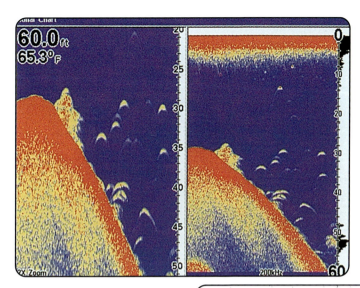

A split screen allows you to see the whole bottom structure (right) while also enlarging the area near the bottom.

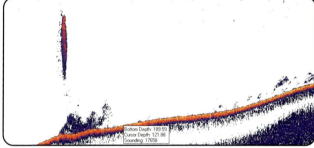

Typical ball of baitfish. The bigger solid marks nearby probably indicate kingfish, while those near the bottom are snapper.

more slowly, the time between travelling over the top and bottom of the peak was much larger and therefore the drop-off was shown to be much shallower and less dramatic. Remember therefore: the faster you go, the sharper and more dramatic the bottom contours will appear.

Of course, the way a boat moves in choppy or rough water will also affect the picture on the screen. Even the flattest sea floor will appear as a rocky reef if the boat is bobbing up and down like a cork.

Grayline

Also known as Greyscale, Whiteline or a number of other proprietary names, this function is used to separate objects near the bottom (such as schools of baitfish) from the actual bottom. It is incredibly useful and should, in normal circumstances, be left

Some modern plotters are so advanced they even show my marina berth!

Gain

The gain function on a sounder acts like a volume control and is best left on automatic unless you are fishing in very deep or very shallow (1–2 m) water. On auto, the gain control will self-adjust the sounder's sensitivity as the depth and amount of life under the waves changes. In deepish water with little sealife, the sensitivity will be high to show up any activity. As soon as the depth decreases or fish are found, the sensitivity will drop back, providing better separation of the various signals and eliminating distortion.

A-scope

Now fitted on a number of sounders, A-scope is like an early warning system of activity below. It appears in a narrow window on the far right of the screen and can be very useful when jigging. A-scopes on some of the more advanced models now also leave a track that remains visible for several seconds.

Colour

Sounders are available in either black and white or colour. Colour sounders generally give a more detailed picture of what is below, especially once you have become familiar with the way they work. Exactly what the various colours represent differs from brand to brand, but the overriding rule is that the deeper the colour, the stronger the signal. There is also quite a difference in performance, and I personally have found the Lowrance Matrix series of sounders to give the best definition and contrast.

switched on all the time (in most brands, this is the default setting).

Grayline also helps to distinguish a hard, rocky bottom (which appears as solid black) from a soft or sandy one (a grey line shows slightly above the real bottom), making it easier to distinguish between pinnacles, clumps of kelp and schools of fish.

Zoom

The zoom function allows you to magnify a particular section of the sea floor, making it easier to see the contours and to check whether there are any fish in the area. Most modern sounders also allow you to split your screen so that you have a normal view in one section and the zoomed image on the other.

Interpreting the Image

Sounders help us identify fish by bouncing a signal off their swim-bladder and sending it back. Unfortunately, our quarry, the snapper, has a very small swim-bladder and is therefore often difficult to spot. (Kingfish and trevally, on the other hand, have quite big swim-bladders and so show up much more clearly.) Snapper sometimes appear as an arch shape, especially if they are quite large, although most appear as a faint vertical or slightly diagonal line, especially if they are over a rocky bottom. A single large fish appears black on top with grey shading underneath, while a school of baitfish usually shows as solid black.

Installing Transducers

When installing a transducer, remember that air is the enemy as air bubbles distort the picture you see and give a totally false picture of what lies below.

Trailer Boats

A properly installed transom-mounted transducer is usually better than a through-hull one as there is less danger of damage from trailer rollers or other objects. As most propellers turn clockwise, mount the transducer on the starboard side, relatively deep in the vee (about 300 mm up from the keel) and clear of any chines, strakes or fittings (look directly forward from the transducer position: there should be nothing ahead but clean hull).

Moored Boats

Boats with stern drives can use transom-

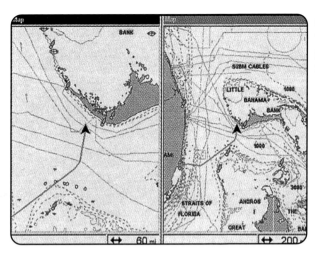

In spilt screen mode you can view your overall position while getting a close up look at the target area.

mounted transducers successfully but all others should fit through-hull models. Many of the same rules apply as for trailer boats: mount about a third of the way forward, in clean water on the starboard side, and away from the line of any seacocks or other fittings.

Using Plotters

GPS plotters have two great advantages: they make it easy to re-find successful spots and they act as a navigation aid in times of low visibility (remember, however, that in such conditions it is always the skipper's responsibility to maintain a look-out as a plotter will not identify objects in your path). Plotters come in all shapes, sizes and budgets, and offer a variety of features. At their most basic, they give a latitude and longitude reading, record waypoints (spots) and show a track from your present position to where you want to go (a little like

steering a car in an arcade game). At their most advanced, they include full-colour digitised charts (just like the paper ones) and plot your position — and all your spots — on screen. Helpfully, they even sound an alarm when you arrive at your destination!

Use the plotter in conjunction with the sounder, especially when you are looking for a good deep-water spot (which is why the two should be mounted as close together as possible on the dash). After identifying a likely looking spot on the chart, 'mark' that spot on the plotter and then use the GPS to find it. Once you are there, use the sounder to check out the contours before deciding where to anchor so that the wind and tide will take your bait and berley to the right place (see 'Deep-water Fishing', page 34). If the spot is a successful one, use the plotter to record it as a waypoint so that it can easily be found again.

Longlining

Used by the commercial fishing industry, longlining is a great way to improve your knowledge of snapper and their movements, and also a great way to get a feed when the fishing is slow, especially in winter and during unfavourable moon phases and small tides. There are a number of 'ready-to-go' longlines available through specialist tackle shops or through ads in the fishing magazines. For those with a bit of a DIY bent, the component parts are also available and relatively easy to assemble. Basically, a longline consists of two droppers (each securely tied to a grapnel), the backbone, the traces and the floats.

The droppers are the lines that hold the longline in place on the seabed. At one end is the grapnel, at the other is the float and, in the middle, is the backbone.

The backbone is the length of line that is clipped on between the two dropper lines and that lies on the bottom of the sea. About every 2 m along its length there is a knot or some other form of stopper. These knots keep the traces, which are clipped on

A longline consists of two droppers (each securely tied to a grapnel), the backbone, the traces and the floats.

to the backbone, apart to ensure that they do not tangle.

The short lengths of trace have a clip at one end (for clipping on to the backbone) and a hook (Japanese longline hooks are the best) at the other. The maximum number of hooks allowed on a longline is 25.

By law, both floats must be marked with the owner's surname and initials. Buy proper floats — plastic bottles are not suitable as they tend to leak and then sink.

Longlines can be a little tricky to use until you get used to them, so make life easy for yourself. Start by setting one on a calm day over a sandy bottom with not too much tidal run. This will help you to get used to the gear, hopefully without tangles or dramas. Never set a longline across a channel. There are three reasons for this: it will be dragged away by the current and foul on every small rock on the bottom; snapper face into the current to feed and

work back and forth across it, so a longline set across the current is a complete waste of time; and retrieving a longline set across a current can be very dangerous.

The biggest mistake most people make when longlining is to use baits that are too big. This probably stems from the 'big bait, big fish' theory and, while that often works well when using a rod or reel, it is no good at all when using a longline. The other fallacy is that a bigger bait lasts longer than a smaller one, giving more chance of a hook-up. Unfortunately, this is not the case either. Snapper feeding on the sand pick at their natural food and big baits can easily be spat out without hooking the fish. Longline baits only need to be about the size of your thumbnail and should only be pushed onto the hook once. Try using a selection of baits — say one-third squid, one-third mullet and one-third piper. Group each type of bait together and remember where on the line you have placed them. This not only covers your bases, but also gives a good indication of what baits you should be using when fishing with a rod and reel.

I have caught good-sized snapper in many of the sandy, shallow bays of the Hauraki Gulf (many surprisingly close to downtown Auckland). Try places you would not normally fish as you will often be amazed at exactly where snapper stop to feed. Do not set longlines in channels with lots of current, on top of reefs or in areas with a lot of passing boats.

After choosing where you want to set your longline, move so that the boat is on the upwind side of the area. Start by

dropping one of the dropper lines until the grapnel touches the bottom. Then let out a few more metres of line to allow for tide and wave action and to ensure the grapnel will stay where it's set. Marking this place on the dropper line, pull it in, attach the float and the backbone and then lower it again.

As the boat moves gently downwind, the backbone is pulled out; attach the traces one at a time as the next gap between the knots appears. Do not be tempted to attach all of the traces to the backbone before setting the longline as this will likely result in an awful tangle. Instead, keep it simple and attach them one at a time.

When all the traces have been clipped on and the backbone has run out fully, give the backbone a final pull to ensure that it is fully stretched out. Then clip on the last dropper line and throw it over the side.

One of the great advantages of using a longline is that the fish are generally still alive and relatively unharmed when you pull them in, so unwanted or undersized fish can be released alive.

Although they often look bright and colourful close up, floats can be difficult to spot from a distance, so be sure to take some transit marks or enter the spot in your GPS before moving away.

Another fallacy about longlines is that the longer they are left, the more chance there is that they will catch fish. Wrong again! After about two hours, all of the remaining baits will have been eaten by sea lice or crabs. Those fish that have been caught will also be under threat from sea lice (which eat them from the inside out) or will have drowned. One of the great advantages of using a longline is that the

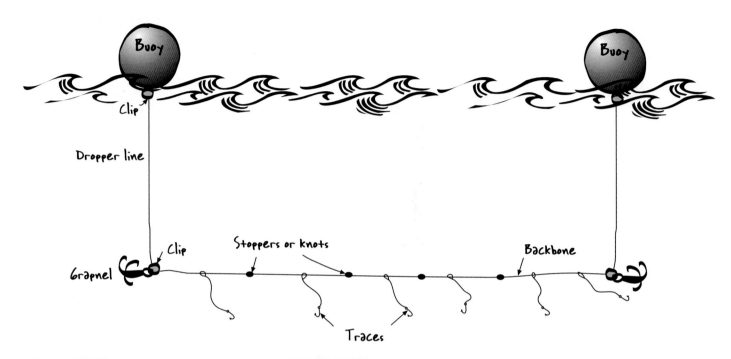

Buoy

Buoy

Clip

Dropper line

Clip

Grapnel

Stoppers or knots

Backbone

Traces

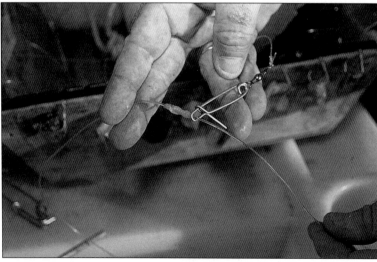

The knots on the backbone keep the traces apart so they do not tangle.

fish are generally still alive and relatively unharmed when you pull them in, so unwanted or undersized fish can be released alive. However, after two hours all the fish will be dead and that's just a waste. I find the ideal time to leave a longline is between an hour and an hour and a half.

Always retrieve the longline from the leeward (downwind) buoy and work upwind. This may seem like making more work but the alternative is worse: you end up drifting back over the still set longline, snagging it on the bottom or around your propeller.

The easiest way to retrieve the longline is to go first to the windward buoy and pull up the dropper line. Remove the float from the

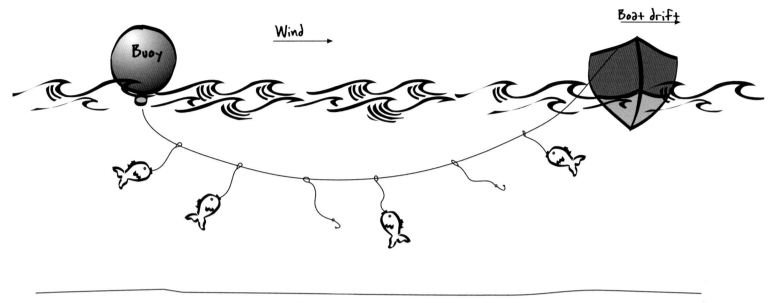

Wind →

Buoy

Boat drift

Bottom

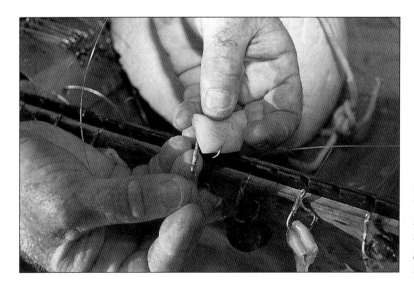

Longline baits only need to be about the size of your thumbnail and should only be pushed onto the hook once.

dropper line and the backbone from the grapnel, and then clip the float directly onto the backbone before throwing it back in the water. Next, head directly to the leeward buoy and pull it in. Detach the grapnel and float and start to wind in the backbone. You will find that the boat and the windward buoy drift gently with the wind. At the same time, the buoy will hold the backbone off the bottom, allowing you to take your time removing the traces (and hopefully the fish!) without fear of snags or tangles.

Undersized or unwanted fish must be released instantly, while those you want to keep can be put straight into a fish bin or livebait tank.

Area ❶ Tiritiri Matangi to A Buoy

Habitat

From Whangaparaoa across to Rakino and down to the entrance to the Rangitoto Channel is an area known as the 'worm beds'. The sea floor here consists mostly of mud and sand with the odd area of low foul and rubble. As this vast stretch of sea floor has a high concentration of worms, crabs and shellfish, it plays a big part in the snapper's annual migration and spawning. Although the bottom appears flat, a close look on the sounder will reveal areas where it rises 50 cm or so; these areas are worth targeting on days of small tides and bad moon phases.

Kotanui Island

Caution: not to be used for navigation.

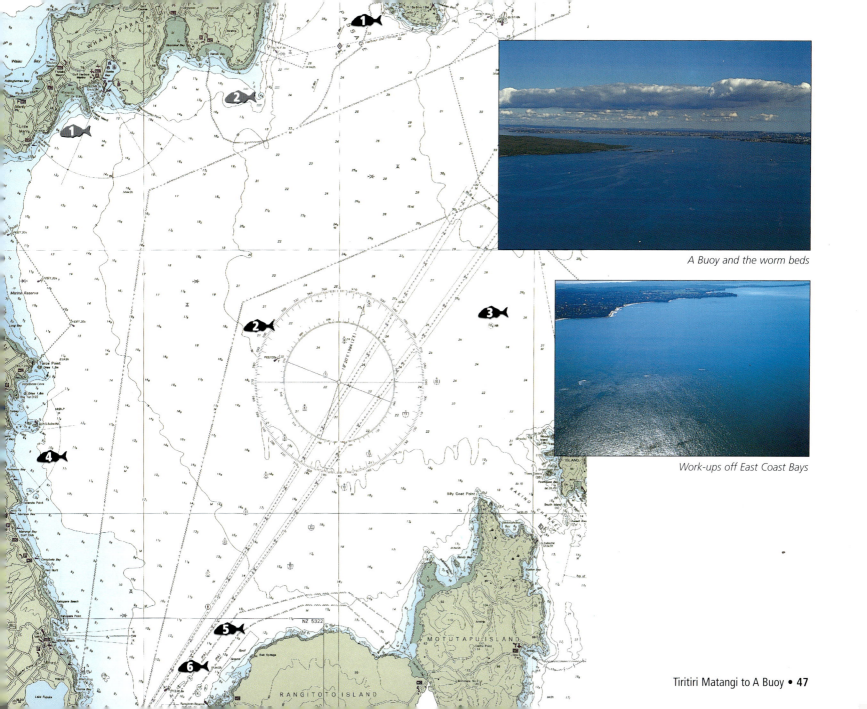

A Buoy and the worm beds

Work-ups off East Coast Bays

Summer

Around September/October, the first schools of snapper appear around Tiri and gradually graze their way south towards the Rangitoto Channel. As food is so prolific and widespread, the snapper can be virtually anywhere and a good sounder is therefore vital in finding them. These pre-spawning snapper are often very slow on the bite, and on days of small tides and bad moon phases I find it pays to set a longline to cover my bases. Fish where the current is strongest and use small half- or strip baits as the snapper will pick at these but leave whole pilchards untouched.

◀ Tiri Channel

There is always good tidal flow through here, and lots of snapper seem to feed just out from the south entrance to the channel.

Ideal conditions Incoming tide with northwesterly to northeasterly winds, or outgoing tide with southwesterly to southerly winds.

◀ The NIWA Buoys

I have always done well in the area just to the east of the NIWA weather buoys. You will need a good sounder and will have to work the area until you find the fish.

Ideal conditions Incoming tide with northwesterly to northeasterly winds, or outgoing tide with southwesterly to southerly winds.

◀ The Wreck

The wreck of a Japanese squid boat is clearly visible on the chart, out off Rakino. This actual wreck is often covered in sand but still seems to hold fish.

Ideal conditions Incoming tide with northerly to northeasterly winds, or outgoing tide with southwesterly to southeasterly winds.

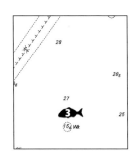

◀ East Coast Bays

Schooling snapper come close inshore along the Bays' coast, which is good for those with a small boat. Even on days when it is too rough to head further out, good fish can still be caught here.

Ideal conditions Incoming tide with northerly winds, or outgoing tide with southerly to southwesterly winds.

◀ The Horse-mussel Beds

There are areas of low foul and horse-mussel beds, visible on the sounder, just under a mile or so out from the Rangitoto shore. This is a good area to pick up 'smokers': snapper around the 3–5-kg mark, with big mouths and jaws strong enough to smash the large horse mussels. Be sure to run your fingers up the trace and line periodically to check for any damage from dragging over the sharp shells.

Ideal conditions Incoming tide with northerly to northeasterly winds, or outgoing tide with southerly to southwesterly winds.

◀ A Buoy

One of the best-known areas of worm beds lies just east of A Buoy in an area of stronger tidal flow. You can't miss it — just look for the several trillion boats anchored there . . .

Ideal conditions Incoming tide with northerly to northeasterly winds, or outgoing tide with southerly to southwesterly winds.

Winter

Around 90 per cent of the school snapper leave the area, making the remaining 10 per cent much harder to find and catch. Most of the resident winter fish head into the local reefs and areas of foul, although a few remain out on the worm beds. However, you will need a good sounder to find them. The best ways to target the winter fish in this area are by straylining around the local rocks and reefs and by setting a longline.

Kotanui Island

This lies just to the southwest of Gulf Harbour Marina and, although hundreds of boats race past it, few stop to fish here. Anchor within casting distance of the kelp line (not the shore), and use plenty of berley and groundbait. The best fishing is on an incoming tide at dusk.

Ideal conditions Incoming tide with northeasterly to easterly winds, or outgoing tide with southwesterly to southerly winds.

The 4.6-Metre Rise

A finger of shallow water (rising from 7 m to just 4.6 m) lies off the southernmost tip of Whangaparaoa. The 4.6-m high point can be surefire at times during the winter.

Ideal conditions Incoming tide with northwesterly to northeasterly winds, or outgoing tide with southwesterly to southerly winds.

Beware Undersea Cables

There are a number of undersea cables that run through the worm bed area and it is illegal to anchor or fish over them. Be sure to check your chart carefully as there are very harsh penalties for those who damage these cables. There is also the possibility of a big shock — some cables carry up to 10,000 volts! Should you somehow foul an anchor on a cable, do not try to free it as you are only likely to damage it (and incur even more expense) or hurt yourself and your crew. Instead, ring **0800 SUBMARINE (0800 782 6274)** *immediately.*

Area ② Rangitoto Light to Billy Goat Point

Habitat

Apart from the two sandy beaches close to the lighthouse, the northern shoreline of Rangitoto is all volcanic lava that extends about 100–200 m out to sea before the bottom becomes sandy again. Although there are quite a few areas of scattered low foul, this sandy bottom is home to some of the snapper's favourite food: worms, crabs and horse mussels. In contrast, the Motutapu shoreline is a mixture of papa (mudstone) rock and lava, with a lot of necklace seaweed (like a string of beads) growing on the papa. Anglers using their depth sounders in fish symbol mode in this area are often fooled into thinking they have discovered a fantastic new spot as these beads appear on the screen as hundreds of fish.

Rangitoto Light

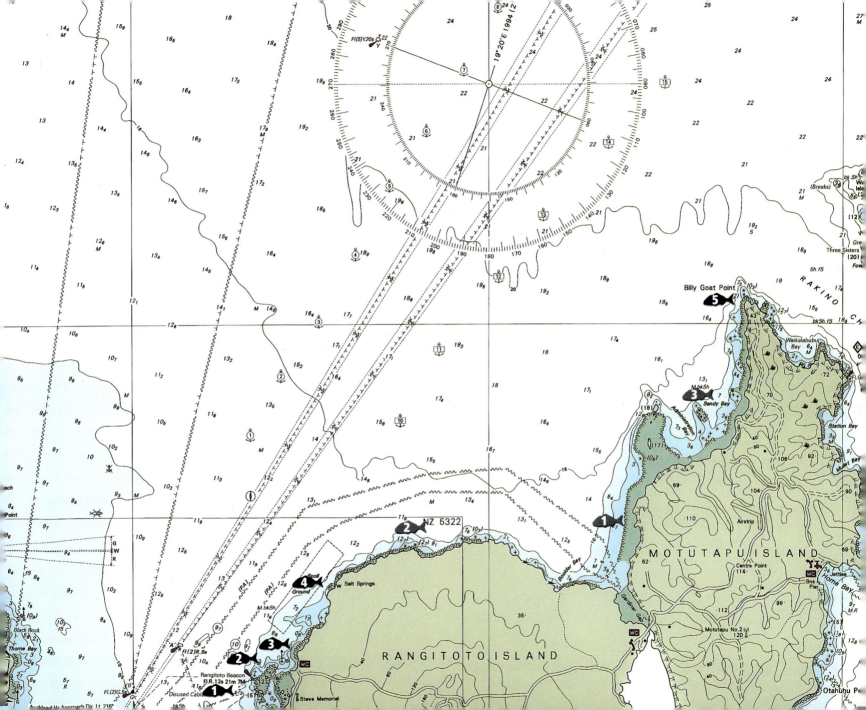

Summer

Snapper do not come in close to the shore in any numbers until late summer, after they have spawned. The only area that consistently fishes well all year round is the stretch from Rangitoto Lighthouse to the headland known as 'Whites', located just past the last sandy beach and recognisable by the dead pohutukawa trees along the shore. The area fishes well all year because of the stronger tidal flows here that bring the fish into the kelp. From mid-February to late April, snapper start feeding in the sand and kelp right along the coast to Billy Goat Point.

Rangitoto Lighthouse Reef is a huge structure separated from the island shoreline by a channel. (Note that it is not considered safe to navigate through this channel.)

1 The Western Side

This can be fished by anchoring at the southern end of the channel and attracting the snapper out to you with berley and groundbait or from the lighthouse back, anchoring just past the northern end of the channel. Both areas have a fast tidal flow and the bottom is rocky.

Ideal conditions Incoming tide with northwesterly to northeasterly winds, or outgoing tide with a southwesterly to southerly wind.

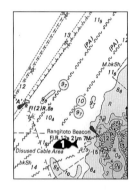

2 The Northern Side

The large volume of water passing through here means that, at some stage, the snapper will come by. Overhead reels and big sinkers are needed. A weighted berley bag, or one that is tied to the anchor line, is worthwhile.

Ideal conditions Incoming tide with northwesterly to northeasterly winds.

3 The Eastern Side

Anchor so that the stern of the boat is facing the reef and far enough away so that your baits can just be cast to the edge of the rocks.

Ideal conditions Incoming tide with easterly to northeasterly winds. (In summer, it is also worth putting out a livebait as many kingfish cruise through this area.)

4 Whites

There is quite a lot of low foul about 50–100 m offshore, and this is easily straylined.

Ideal conditions Incoming tide with a northerly to easterly wind, or outgoing tide with southerly to westerly winds (best at dawn or dusk in late April).

Administration Bay (Motutapu Island) has a clean bottom that is good for drift fishing and jigging. Alternatively, set a longline between the outermost island and Billy Goat Point.

5 Billy Goat Point

There are a lot of rocks and kelp on the western side of this point. Big butterflied baits work well at dusk.

Ideal conditions Outgoing tide with a westerly to southerly wind.

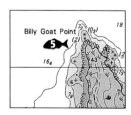

Winter

Owing to the vast areas of seaweed, which are home to crabs, snails and limpets, a lot of snapper winter over in this area, occasionally moving out to the low foul areas. A lot of berley, groundbait and patience are often needed to bring the snapper on the bite, although the area will generally fish well after a strong northerly storm.

Summer spots 1–5 fish well in the winter, too, and the same ideal conditions apply.

① Gardiner Gap

Zigzag your way out to sea and then back to the outer island of Administration Bay. There are patches (some quite big) of low foul covered with seaweed. Anchor back from these so that your baits land close to the kelp but not in it. Use plenty of berley. Dawn and dusk fishing are best, but be prepared to hook some big stingrays.

Ideal conditions Incoming tide with northerly to northwesterly winds, or outgoing tide with southerly to westerly winds.

② Awash Rocks

Heading east, about halfway along Rangitoto, the shoreline curves in and there are two rocks that are awash at low tide. Anchor to the east of the small headland and strayline back using smaller, half-baits.

Ideal conditions Incoming tide with northeasterly winds.

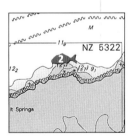

③ Administration Bay

There is a large reef structure at the western end of the bay. Fish back into the structure using lots of berley, groundbait and patience.

Ideal conditions Incoming tide with northerly to easterly winds (northeastern side), or outgoing tide with southerly to westerly winds (southwestern side).

Administration Bay

Area ③ Rangitoto Channel

Habitat

The Rangitoto Channel is very popular with boats of all sizes in summer, and consequently is not without its hazards. As the main shipping lane into Auckland it is a very busy commercial waterway, and so boats are not permitted to anchor in the actual channel. There are also important telecommunications and power cables running through this area (clearly marked on the chart) and it is not permitted to anchor or fish over these. The sea floor here is a real mixture of mud, broken shell and rocky, low-lying reefs, and the strong tidal flows bring lots of nutrients into the upper harbour for the baitfish. There is plenty of food here for the snapper, too: crabs, worms and shellfish in the channels, and crabs, limpets and snails on the kelpy Rangitoto shoreline and on the seaweed-covered reefs. However, this is not a good place for longlines as there are too many rocks and too much tidal flow and boat traffic.

Browns Bay Reef

Caution: not to be used for navigation.

Summer

The first schools of snapper arrive in early November, feeding up and down the channel until late December. They then move further in, sometimes as far as Hobsonville (where there are good feeding grounds) or beyond. In late March or early April, as the sea and air temperatures begin to drop, they move out again. The early snapper can be frustratingly hard to catch, often refusing to feed at all. When this happens, it can be worth pulling up anchor and drift fishing with baited ledger or flasher rigs instead (you tend to lose a bit of gear in the foul, but the snapper are more likely to react to a moving bait). On small tides in November and December, smaller cut or half-baits work best. From January through to April (except on small tides), use whole pilchards and squid, rigged with keeper hooks (see 'Successful Straylining Rigs', page 22).

①◄ A Buoy

I am constantly amazed at how many snapper pass between A Buoy and the lighthouse. Find them by zigzagging across the area with the sounder set on zoom, and either drift fish using jigs, ledger or flasher rigs, or anchor and use a running sinker rig with a 1-m-long trace.

Ideal conditions Incoming tide with northwesterly to northeasterly winds, or outgoing tide with southwesterly to southeasterly winds.

②◄ Number 2 Buoy

About 100–200 m on the Rangitoto side of Number 2 Buoy is a series of rises and falls where snapper often rest out of the current. Ledger and running sinker rigs work best here. Do not, of course, anchor on the channel side of the buoy.

Ideal conditions Incoming tide with northwesterly to northerly winds, or outgoing tide with southeasterly to easterly winds.

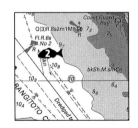

③◄ Rangitoto Lighthouse

Just south of the lighthouse and about 100 m from the rocks, the bottom undulates quite a lot. Strong tide runs necessitate 6–8-oz sinkers at full flood. Use a running sinker rig with either a 50-cm- or 2-m-long

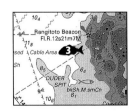

trace, depending on the strength of the tide.

Ideal conditions Incoming tide with northwesterly to westerly winds, or outgoing tide with southeasterly to easterly winds.

④◄ Number 2 Buoy to the Barges

A current line, caused by a reef further back, runs from the Barges to Number 2 Buoy on an outgoing tide. Start at Number 2 Buoy and zigzag into the tide toward the barge area until the snapper appear on the sounder. Head further up until the tide turns, then anchor back towards (not on top of!) the fish. Best in February and March.

Ideal conditions Outgoing tides with southeasterly to easterly winds.

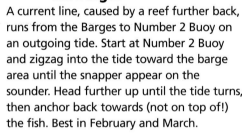

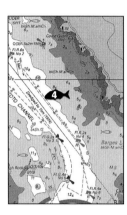

⑤◄ Drifting in the Channel

Snapper often go off the bite at slack water, and it can be worthwhile drift fishing in the channel at this time as long as there is no shipping in the area. Always keep the engine running so that you can move in a hurry, and keep an eye on the sounder to learn about the area and the way the snapper move about in it.

Winter

In winter, most of the snapper move out of the channel and closer to the shore among the rocks, reefs and kelp. In big storms that last for several days (such as Cyclone Bola in 1988), snapper will also come inshore to shelter behind Rangitoto. From Milford to North Head, there are a few patches of small reefs and isolated rocks that all hold resident fish over the winter. Straylining with small baits and lots of berley, groundbait and patience will get results as long as the wind and tide are running in the same direction.

 Browns Bay Reef

Anchor just beyond casting distance to the kelp line and berley heavily. Best at change of light.

Ideal conditions Incoming tide with northwesterly to northeasterly winds, or outgoing tide with southerly to southeasterly winds.

Black Rock

Another good dawn or dusk spot that benefits from a steady stream of berley and groundbait.

Ideal conditions Incoming tide with northwesterly to northeasterly winds, or outgoing tide with southerly to southeasterly winds.

Narrow Neck

There is lots of foul ground in the area between St Leonards and Narrow Neck beaches. Choose one spot and strayline through the whole tide with berley and groundbait.

Ideal conditions Incoming tide with northwesterly to northeasterly winds, or outgoing tide with southerly to southeasterly winds.

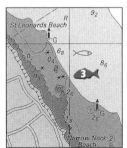

Coastguard Buoy (1)

This yellow buoy is permanently moored in the first bay around from the lighthouse. It is used by coastguard rescue boats and so other vessels cannot tie up to it. Anchor just north of and about 100 m out from the buoy. Cast well back to the foul ground.

Ideal conditions Outgoing tide with southerly to southwesterly winds.

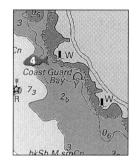

Coastguard Buoy (2)

Anchor 100 m out from and to the south of the buoy. Cast well astern (to the edge of the foul) and use lots of berley.

Ideal conditions Incoming tide with northwesterly to northerly winds.

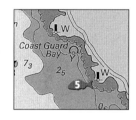

The White Marker

There is a small headland with a white marker on the Rangitoto shore just inside Number 4 Buoy. Anchor directly uptide of the marker in shallow water, with the stern of the boat facing the headland.

Ideal conditions Incoming tide with northwesterly winds.

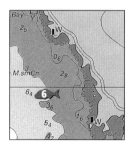

Area ④ North Head to Browns Island

Habitat

This area tends to be overlooked by many anglers as they race past it on their way to other spots further out. Yet it is an ideal area for those with smaller boats as many of the good fishing spots are close to shore and work well in both summer and winter. There are three distinct tidal flows in this area: the Rangitoto Channel, the Motuihe Channel and the Tamaki Strait. It is worth spending some time studying the effects of these flows as there are a number of back eddies that allow you to fish in places that, at first glance, would appear to suffer from unfavourable wind-against-tide conditions. The open areas of water here largely feature a sandy bottom, rich in sealife such as crabs, shrimps and shellfish. In contrast, the many reefs and rocky shorelines are largely of volcanic origin, where a variety of seaweeds provide a healthy covering. This is an ideal habitat for limpets, mussels, oysters and the like — the favourite winter menu of the resident snapper.

Browns Island

Caution: not to be used for navigation.

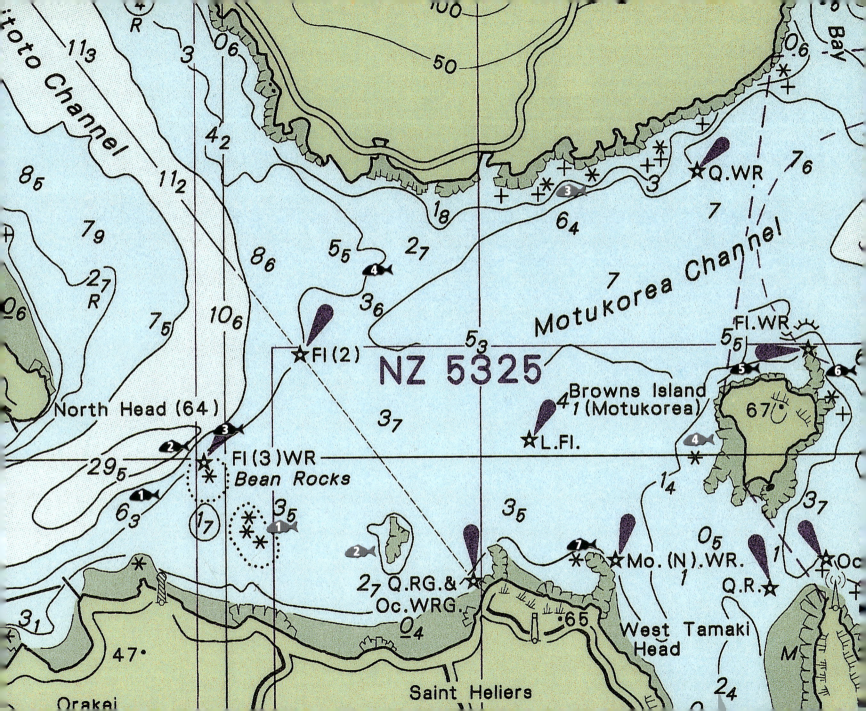

Summer

Once the snapper have mostly completed their early season spawning, large numbers move here in early January, feeding across the whole area. Although the bottom appears featureless, the area does hold a lot of food and, when you are passing through, it is well worth looking at the sounder and using the opportunity to build up your local knowledge.

1 Orakei Wharf

Use the sounder to find where the bottom drops away, then anchor so that you are fishing down the drop-off that lies about a third of the way between the wharf and Bean Rock Lighthouse.

Ideal conditions Incoming tide with northerly to northwesterly winds, or outgoing tide with southerly to southwesterly winds.

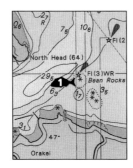

2 Bean Rock (City Side)

The seabed drops off steeply on this side of the lighthouse, and snapper are often found on the lower slopes and at the bottom of the drop-off.

Ideal conditions Incoming tide with northerly to northeasterly winds, or outgoing tide with westerly to southerly winds.

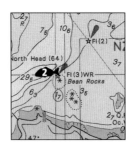

3 Bean Rock (Northern Side)

The flat bottom on the north side of the lighthouse often holds schools of fish. Although they tend to move on relatively quickly, the area can be worth a look when you are passing.

Ideal conditions Incoming tide with northerly to easterly winds, or outgoing tide with southwesterly to westerly winds.

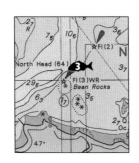

4 Northern Leading Light to Rangitoto Shoreline

This large area of flat sand has lots of patches of low foul and is the official anchorage for barges. Best results are achieved in late March and throughout April by straylining at dawn or dusk.

Ideal conditions Incoming tide with southerly to westerly winds or outgoing tide with east to southeast winds.

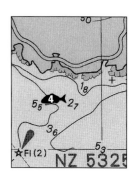

5 and 6 Browns Island

The northern and eastern sides of the island feature a lot of low foul and reasonably strong tidal flows. Consequently, the stretch is best fished when the wind and tide are running in the same direction. The nature of the landscape means that berley and groundbait are particularly effective at attracting bigger fish.

Ideal conditions Incoming tide with northerly to easterly winds, or outgoing tide with southwesterly to westerly winds.

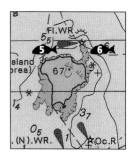

7 Tamaki River

A small lighthouse on the city side of the reef structures is an ideal spot in strong southwesterly winds and is also quite sheltered.

Ideal conditions Outgoing tide with southwesterly winds.

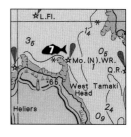

Winter

Resident snapper winter over close to the shoreline in this area. They feed around the kelp and rocks, and are often found in water as shallow as 1 m. It is essential that the wind and tide are running together and that you use lots of berley and groundbait, along with a good dollop of patience (it won't happen immediately but it will happen . . .).

🐟 West Bastion Reef

This large area of reef is home to some big snapper. Try different areas as this is a big reef.

Ideal conditions Incoming tide with northerly to easterly winds (eastern side), or outgoing tide with westerly to southerly winds (western side).

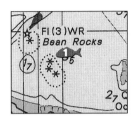

Bean Rock (West Bastion Reef)

🐟 East Bastion Reef

This semi-circular reef runs north to south. Anchor within casting distance of the kelp and strayline back to the shore.

Ideal conditions Incoming tide with northwesterly to southwesterly winds (eastern side), or outgoing tide with easterly to southeasterly winds (western side).

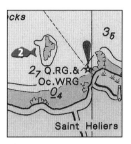

🐟 Rangitoto Shoreline

From west of the main wharf all the way down to Islington Bay, this area is strewn with kelp-covered rocks and small reefs. Fish back into these areas when the wind and tide are running in the same direction.

Ideal conditions Wind and tide running in the same direction.

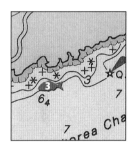

🐟 Browns Island

The huge kelp beds on the western side of the island can be fished at all stages of the tide.

Ideal conditions Incoming tide with westerly to northerly winds, or outgoing tide with westerly to southerly winds.

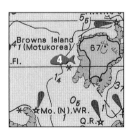

Area ⑤ Motuihe Channel and Sergeant Channel

Habitat

These channels are two of the most fished stretches of water in the Hauraki Gulf, and many thousands of snapper are caught here over the summer months. The snapper — both before and after they have spawned — have to run the gauntlet of hundreds of anglers in order to reach the food-rich areas of the Tamaki Strait and the inner harbour. The channel floors largely consist of sand and shell with some rock and papa. There are crabs and worms here, as well as numerous baitfish, which feed on the nutrients in the strong tidal flows. Schools of kahawai also chase these baitfish and, in summer, so do the kingfish.

Rock structure beneath the water tower, Motuihe Island

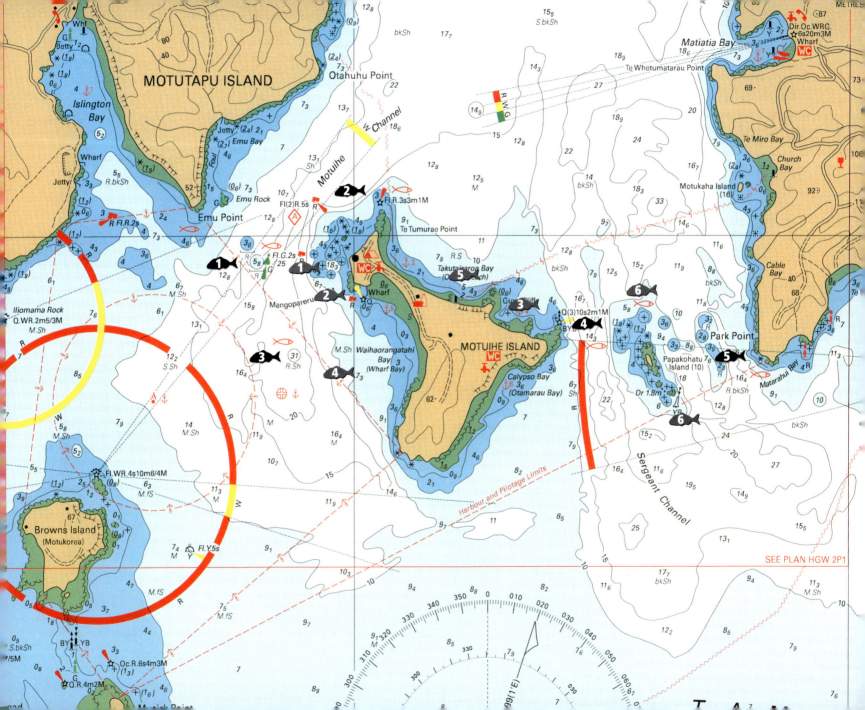

Summer

By early November, a lot of school snapper are feeding here, moving back and forth through the channels. As more and more snapper arrive, the competition for food forces many out onto the surrounding banks. Tidal run plays a huge part in the feeding habits of these fish, and they will often stop eating altogether as slack water approaches. Drift fishing with baited flasher or ledger rigs can often be worthwhile during the turn of the tide as the snapper are quite aggressive toward a moving bait.

❶ Motuihe Channel Rocks

There are two rocks (3.6 m and 5.8 m) to the north of the green channel markers. These often fish best on an incoming tide using a ledger or running sinker rig with mullet or squid.

Ideal conditions Incoming tide with northerly to northeasterly winds, or outgoing tide with southerly to southwesterly winds.

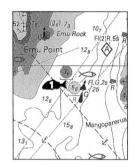

❷ Motuihe Reef

This reef extends northwards from the northern end of Motuihe. Anchor just south of the red marker on the channel side on an incoming tide, and use long traces on a running sinker rig. There are also lots of trevally here in late summer.

Ideal conditions Incoming tide with northwesterly to northeasterly winds, or outgoing tide with southerly to southwesterly winds.

❸ The 31-Metre Hole

Located southwest of the Motuihe wharf, this hole generally attracts lots of boats as it fishes well in all tide directions. Flasher and ledger rigs with a cocktail of pilchard and squid work best.

Ideal conditions Incoming tide with northerly to northwesterly winds, or outgoing tide with southerly to southwesterly winds.

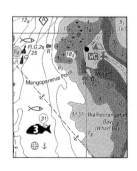

❹ Sergeant's Hole

Between the easternmost point of Motuihe and Crusoe Island, the channel drops to 16.7 m before rising again to 14.3 m. This area can offer dynamite fishing at dusk in late summer, with fish up to 5 kg. The incoming tide seems best.

Ideal conditions Incoming tide with northerly quarter winds, or outgoing tide with southerly quarter winds.

Sergeant's Channel

❺ Park Point

To the west of the point the bottom drops to 3.9 m before rising back to 2.3 m. At times it is wall to wall with boats here, all of them catching fish. A running sinker rig with a long trace or ledger rigs are best.

Ideal conditions Incoming tide with northerly to northwesterly winds, or outgoing tide with southeasterly to southerly winds.

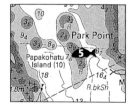

Winter

Most snapper have left this area by late May, when the water temperature has dropped and there is a chill in the wind. However, some do winter over in the reefs and along the rocky shoreline. You generally need to use berley and groundbait to bring these resident snapper on the bite, and it pays to choose one spot and stay there through the whole tide. On occasions, especially just after a big storm has stirred up the bottom, snapper also feed in the channels.

1 Under the Water Tower

There are always a few snapper in among the rocks and reefs under the water tower on Motuihe. However, take lots of care as the tidal flows here are very strong and there are a lot of barely submerged rocks.

Ideal conditions Incoming tide with northerly to northeasterly winds, or outgoing tide with southwesterly winds.

2 The Red Buoy

There is shallow water and a kelpy bottom inside the red marker buoy near the wharf on Motuihe. An outgoing tide will distribute a good berley trail into a very reefy area, but patience is needed as it can take up to two hours for the fish to come on the bite.

Ideal conditions Outgoing tide with southwesterly to southerly winds.

3 Snapper Bay

This is the last bay on the eastern side of Motuihe, with a reef extending from its far end. Anchor well inside and to the west of the reef marker so that the stern of the boat faces the reef. Cast a pattern of baits to the edge of the kelp.

Ideal conditions Incoming tide with westerly to southwesterly winds.

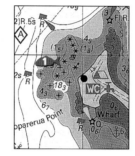

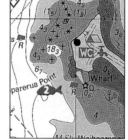

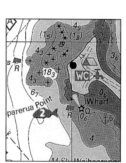

4 The 10-Metre Drop-off

South of the ski lane on the western side of Motuihe, in a depth of 10 m, is one of the most consistent spots I know for catching pan-size snapper. Fish on the edge of the drop-off.

Ideal conditions Any tide and any winds!

5 Ocean Beach

Look for the area of cliffs midway along Ocean Beach and head directly in until a kelp bed appears on the sounder. Just outside the kelp line is a great place to set a longline.

Ideal conditions Any tide is okay, but a southerly quarter wind will make it easier to retrieve the gear.

6 Papakohatu Island (Crusoe)

This area is very foul and snapper hold in the rocks and reef all winter. Best results come fom fishing a whole tide flow with heaps of groundbait and berley. Strayline back to the kelp line.

Ideal conditions Incoming tide (northside) north to northwest winds, or outgoing tide (southside) south to southeast winds.

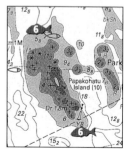

Area ⑥ Tamaki Strait

Habitat

The Tamaki Strait is a large area of fairly shallow water, devoid of any reef structures and containing just a few holes. The bottom consists mainly of sand, although there are some areas of sandy mud and broken shell. The entire strait is rich with crabs, worms, shellfish and shrimps, making it a very important area for snapper, which move here after they have spawned to build up condition for the coming winter. The abundant supply of food combined with the featureless terrain means that snapper are found feeding throughout the area.

Rocky Bay

Caution: not to be used for navigation.

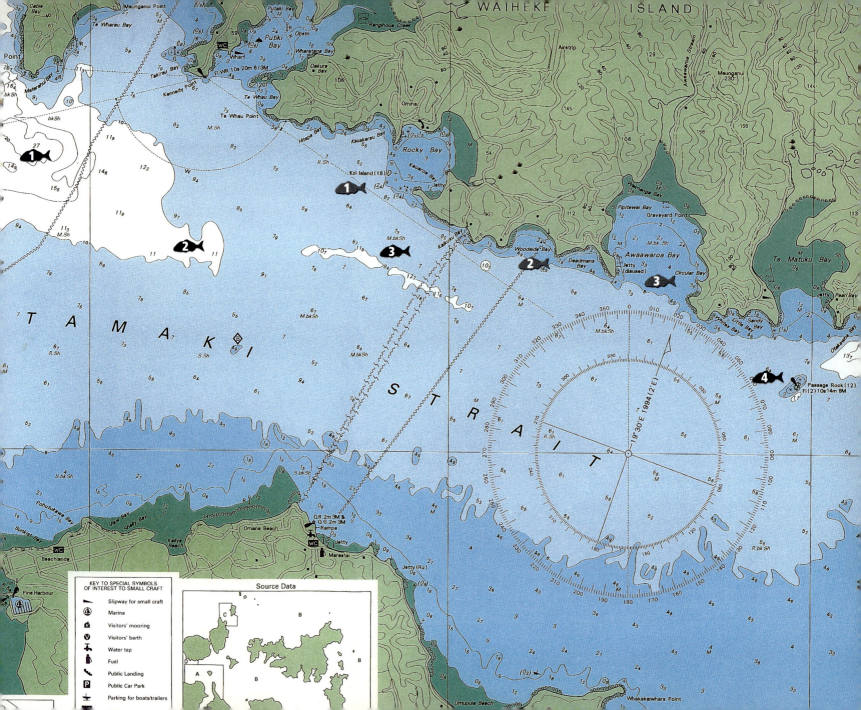

Summer

After spawning, snapper tend to move into the Tamaki Strait in large numbers. They usually arrive in December and stay until March or April, when they move out for the winter. The predominant wind direction here is southwesterly, so an outgoing tide will ensure that both the boat and the fishing lines are lying in the same direction. With the boat moving at a relatively low speed, use the depth sounder's zoom function to find the fish (see 'Sounders and Plotters', page 38). Look for fish marks hard on the bottom and then move downcurrent to determine the size and spread of the school. If the school seems worth fishing, move back over it and anchor so that the marks are just starting to show under the stern of the boat. Be sure to turn off the sounder. Using berley in this area will pay big dividends. The best way to do this is with a weighted berley bag set just off the bottom and another floating off the stern. This will create a substantial berley trail that will attract fish from miles around. Chopped-up groundbait (see 'Berley and Groundbait', page 32) should also be tossed astern regularly to hold the fish close to the baits. This area is best fished using the straylining method (see 'Straylining', page 26), with a small sinker running directly down onto the hook. Cast the bait well astern and allow the current to take it down. If you prefer to use a trace, make it a short one so that it doesn't limit your ability to cast a decent distance. It is much easier to detect even the very smallest of bites when the baits have been cast well astern. This area is very popular in summer and the fish can become a bit bait-shy, so try areas with little passing traffic. The best fishing is often at dawn or dusk. In winds under 15 knots, drift fishing (see 'Deep-water Fishing', page 34) is also a good way to fish this area as it allows you to cover a lot of ground in a relatively short time.

1 The 27-Metre Hole

Directly south of Park Point is a large hole that varies in depth from between 24 m and 27 m. I have always had the most success in the deepest part, drift fishing with baited flasher or ledger rigs.

Ideal conditions Incoming tide with northerly winds, or outgoing tide with southerly to southwesterly winds.

2 The 11-Metre Finger

Due south of Kennedy Point is a finger of deeper water, bottoming out at 11 m in an area about 9 m deep.

Ideal conditions Incoming tide with westerly winds, or outgoing tide with easterly winds.

3 The Trenches

Directly south of Rocky Bay is a series of trenches that drop from 6–7 m down to 12 m. Cast well back astern using small sinkers.

Ideal conditions Incoming tide with westerly winds, or outgoing tide with easterly winds.

4 Passage Rock

Find the school fish on the sounder and then anchor so that you can cast back to the fish. Heavier sinkers will probably be required as the tidal flows are often strong.

Ideal conditions Incoming tide with northerly to northeasterly winds, or outgoing tide with westerly to southwesterly winds.

Winter

Although the vast majority of snapper move out of this area during the winter, good numbers do choose to remain. However, these fish are a lot harder to catch, especially in the open water. This is a good time to use a longline (see 'Longlining', page 42) to improve your chances. A lot of the snapper that do winter over here take up residence in one of the many bays along the Waiheke shoreline. They do this so that they can forage on the mussels, crabs and limpets that live on the rocks and kelp, and they are often found within casting distance of the shore. Try to fish across a whole tide as it will often take a few hours for the fish to take a bait. Berley and regular groundbaiting are absolutely vital for winter fishing in shallow water. Use the berley bag on the surface and be sure to shake it regularly to ensure a consistent, inviting trail. As in the summer, straylining is the best method, with just a little or no sinker required. Cast away from the boat, at varying angles and distances, setting a pattern of baits until you find the fish.

 Rocky Bay

Fish the rocks and reef structures on the starboard side as you enter the bay.

Ideal conditions Incoming tide with southerly to southwesterly winds.

 Woodside Bay

Fish the kelp beds at the western end, from the headland right into the bay. Anchor a little way out and cast back to the kelp line.

Ideal conditions Incoming tide with southeasterly winds, or outgoing tide with westerly to southwesterly winds.

 Awaawaroa Bay

Fish the mussel farm, which acts like a natural reef. This large, open bay is also home to lots of shellfish and baitfish, and a longline works well here, too.

Ideal conditions Incoming tide with easterly winds.

Awaawaroa Bay mussel farm

Area ⑦ Rakino Channel (Including Middle Ground)

Waikalabubu Bay, Motutapu Island

Habitat

A vast amount of water passes through this area and consequently the tidal flows can be quite strong at times. The bottom is basically sand, except for small amounts of rock and reef extending a short way off the shoreline of Motutapu. These waters are very rich in nutrients, and baitfish congregate here in large numbers. In summer, the baitfish have been so thick that my depth-sounder bottom alarm (set at 2 m) has gone off when the true depth was over 19 m! The baitfish are sometimes worked up by the kahawai and kingfish in such numbers that snapper rise to the surface to get among them. The sandy bottom holds lots of crabs, worms and shellfish, including scallops (if you know where to look). With this abundance of food, it is little wonder that the snapper fishing is so good in both summer and winter.

Caution: not to be used for navigation.

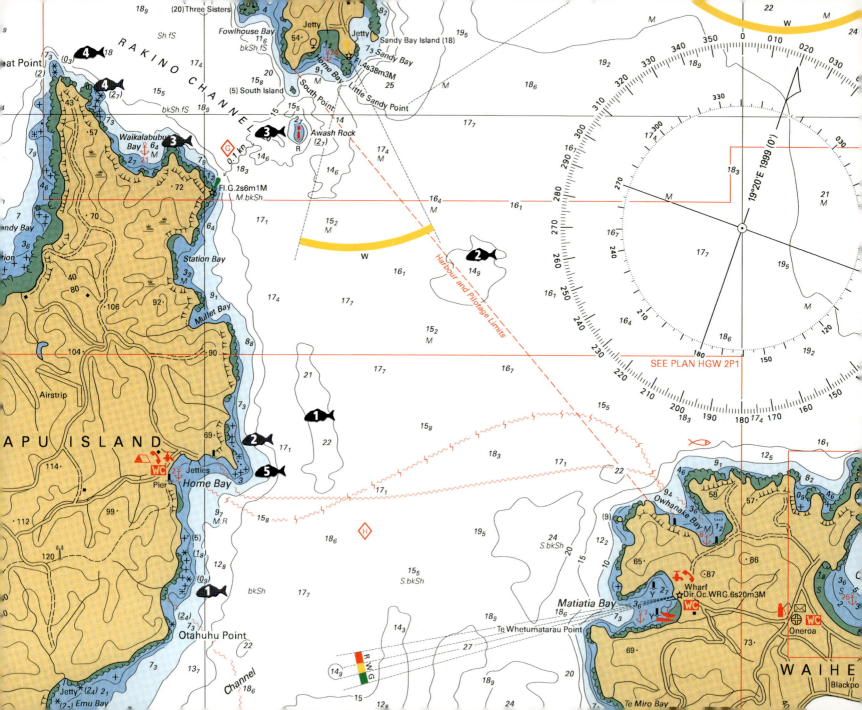

Summer

Generally speaking, by late October or early November pre-spawning snapper start to assemble in this area. These schools move about a lot, so it is important to monitor their movements constantly. Like all pre-spawning snapper, they can be fussy on what, where and when they eat, and it can be very frustrating to see fish on a sounder and then discover that they won't take a bait. At times like this, I drift fish as moving baits often fire the snapper into action. I try to cover my bases by using three different rigs — baited flasher rig, ledger rig (with mixed baits) and a running rig set well out from the boat. With a clean, sandy bottom there is little chance of lines snagging, and by drifting I can cover a lot of ground and different depths in a fairly short time. Often, very few fish will appear on the bottom of the main channel between mid-morning and mid-afternoon. However, as the sun falls, the snapper start to mass up and get into feeding mode. I have spent many a hard day's fishing with little to show for it until about 5.30 p.m., and then, in just half an hour, have put enough in the bin to head home.

1 Home Bay

On the chart, find the finger of deep water that lies northeast of Home Bay. This is an ideal spot for drift fishing. Run up and down the edges and ends of this hole as the best fishing is often on its banks rather than in the middle.

Ideal conditions Incoming tide with northerly winds, or outgoing tide with southerly winds.

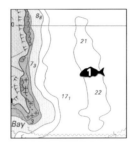

2 The Middle Ground

Northeast of the deep-water finger mentioned above is what I call the Middle Ground, a featureless, flat, sandy bottom rising 1–2 m above the surrounding area. The snapper are often widely spread here and only small marks show on the sounder. Start by drift fishing and, once you get on to the fish, anchor up with a berley bag set down near the bottom.

Ideal conditions Incoming tide with northwesterly to northeasterly winds, or outgoing tide with southwesterly to southeasterly winds.

3 Rakino Channel Between Awash Rock and Motutapu

A lot of fish pass through here; however, although there is a 20-m hole, there is no

other structure or reason for them to stop, so fishing can be good one moment and then dead for some time, until the next school passes. Put a livebait down on the bottom as John Dory can often be found here in numbers.

Ideal conditions Incoming tide with northwesterly winds, or outgoing tide with southwesterly winds.

4 Billy Goat Point

From Billy Goat Point to the northern end of Rakino the bottom is clean and sandy. This is an ideal place to set a longline, drift fish or jig under any birds that are working the water.

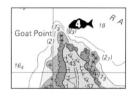

5 Home Bay Reef

This reef extends quite a way east from the headland and the tidal run over the area is strong enough to hold a boat against the wind. Use the sounder to locate the snapper and then fish back to them, not on top of them. If they go off the bite, they may have moved and you will have to repeat the process.

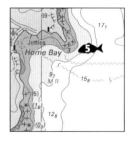

Ideal conditions Incoming tide with northerly to northeasterly winds, or outgoing tide with southwesterly to southerly winds.

Winter

Although the vast majority of snapper leave the Hauraki Gulf in winter, this is one area where the summer spots can fish well all year round. A lot of snapper move in close among the rocks and kelp along the Motutapu shoreline, from Otahuhu Point right around to Billy Goat Point. When fishing this shoreline, make sure the wind and tide are running in the same direction as the tidal flows close inshore are strong. Be prepared to lose a fair amount of terminal tackle in the foul.

1 Otahuhu Point

In the middle of the bay north of the point is a large area of low foul covered in kelp. Anchor back from the rocks and cast to the kelp line. Berley and groundbait are a must.

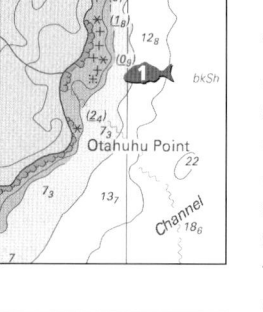

Ideal conditions Incoming tide with northwesterly to northeasterly winds, or outgoing tide with southerly to southeasterly winds. An outgoing tide fishes best.

2 Home Bay

Just north of the point is a very rocky area that often holds fish. Be aware of the strong back eddy on the outgoing tide as this makes it very difficult to fish.

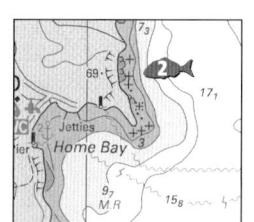

Ideal conditions Incoming tide with a northerly to northeasterly wind.

3 Waikalabubu (1)

The southeastern end of the bay hooks around and features a large, exposed reef structure. There are two alternatives: on an outgoing tide with easterly winds, anchor about 60 m off the broken rock on the southern side and strayline back into the shore; or, on an incoming tide with westerly to northwesterly winds, anchor about 30 m off the gap about midway down the northern side of the reef and strayline back into the rock.

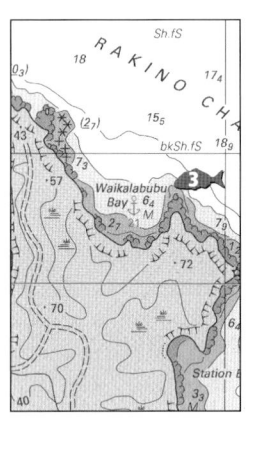

Ideal conditions Incoming tide with westerly to northwesterly winds, or outgoing tide with easterly to southeasterly winds.

4 Waikalabubu (2)

There is a large submerged reef structure at the very northern end of the bay, running right up to Billy Goat Point, and care must be taken when close in here. Some good-size snapper lurk about in these rocks, but be warned: this is an area where time, berley and effort are required as the fishing can be very slow at times.

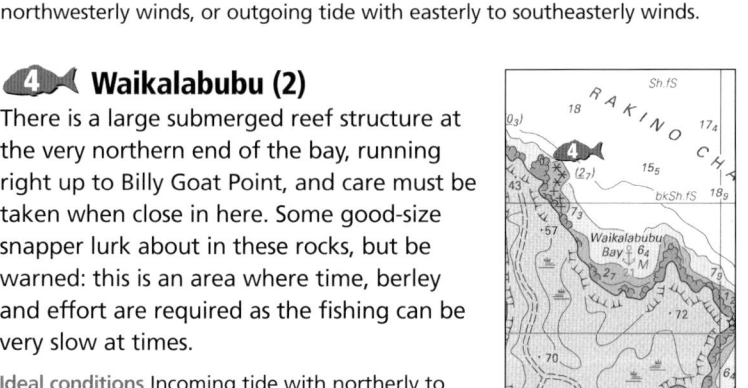

Ideal conditions Incoming tide with northerly to easterly winds, or outgoing tide with southerly to southeasterly winds.

Shoreline north of Home Bay

Area  Rakino Island

Habitat

The Rakino Island shoreline is dotted with small bays and rocky outcrops. The strong flow of clean water and nutrients that passes around the island promotes kelp growth, which in turn means there are plenty of limpets, snails and kina for the snapper. There are also a number of small islands around the shoreline that provide shelter for snapper in rough conditions. Quite close to shore, the sea floor drops down to a sandy 20–25-m bottom that is home to crabs, shellfish and worms.

West Bay, Rakino Island

Caution: not to be used for navigation.

M

24

24

3

22

24

22

14₉

17₇

6₇

15₅

11₆

North East Bay

22

7₃

0₉

4₉

9₁

North East Point

22

18₃

60·

4

11₆

25

22

8₂

12₈

1₅

5₅

Red Bullock Bay

19₂ bkSh

3₆

6₄ (25)Woody Island

62·

2

24

19₅ (Breaks)

3₆

13₇

7₃

0₃ 0₃

22

2

9₇

5 Woody Bay

0₉

25₅

4₃

10 7₃ 5

4₆

3

20

20

7₃10

1₂

9₇

6₇

Maori Garden Bay

4₃

(12)

0₃

West Bay

4₃

14₃ M

21

2₇ 1₂

4 3₂ 23

65·

25

7₃

3₃

9₇Greenbush Bay

0₉ 4

4₉

16₁

18₆

(20)Three Sisters

1₅

1₈

9₁

19₅

Fowlhouse Bay

11₆

54·

1₈ Jetty

Jetty

Sandy Bay Island(18)

19₂

2₇

0₆ 24

Sandy Bay

25

bkSh.fS

16₄

South Point

1₂

3₆

7₃

Fl.4s38m3M

17₄

20

4₆

9₁ Home Bay

Pohutukawa Bay

Little Sandy Point

25

19₅ M

17₇

15₈

7₆

M

(5) South Island

13₄

20

18₉

17₁

15₅

14

15

14

15

17

kSh.fS

15₈

15₈

15

10

2₇

15

Harbour and Pilotage

18₉

12₅

17₁

15₂

7₃ Awash Rock

15₈

17₄

1₅

0₁kn

R

14₆

13₁

M

17₁

0₉

7₉ 12₃

Rakino Island

1

O C H A N N E L

Rakino Island looking towards Little Barrier

Sandy Bay Island

Summer

The school snapper coming in to spawn will often hold around Rakino, waiting for the water to warm up before they move further inshore. There are times when my sounder has shown massive schools of snapper — up to 5 m thick! — on the bottom. These schools move about, so spend time using the sounder to locate them. While these schools of spawning snapper can often be bait-shy, drifting a baited flasher or ledger rig can get their attention.

1 Tubby's Spot

Line up the northern end of Rakino with the southern end of Otata Island (in the Noises group), and then, looking back down the Rakino Channel, line up the Three Sisters and South Island; you should be in approximately 21 m of water. Although the area is flat, the tidal pressure always seems to bring the snapper past at some stage of the tide.

Ideal conditions An incoming tide with northwesterly to northeasterly winds is best, or an outgoing tide with southwesterly to southeasterly winds.

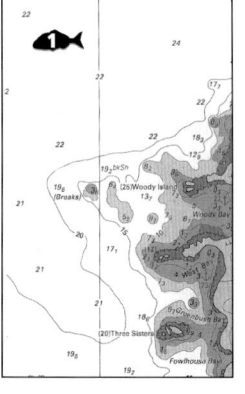

2 Woody Bay Reef

This is a large area of reef that rises to a depth of 5 m, with a rock to the west (3.6 m) that breaks the surface in a big swell. The reef fishes best at change of light, especially in the evening. Always fish back on to the reef — I only fish on top of it at slack water, when I strayline back down the edges with an unweighted bait.

Ideal conditions Incoming tide with northerly to northeasterly winds (north side), or outgoing tide with southerly to southwesterly winds (south side).

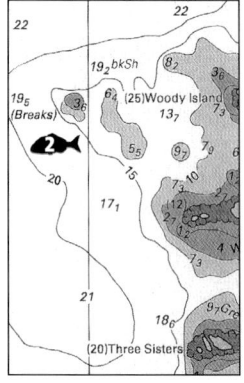

3 North of North East Bay

The bottom runs out to a 14.9-m pinnacle and then drops off to 22 m. On the other side of this line are depths of 15.5 m and 11.6 m. Watching the sounder, work your way along one side of the line and then down the other. Don't stop at the first sign of fish, but get a picture of the whole area in your mind first. The best sign is sometimes found on the 22-m drop-off.

Ideal conditions Incoming tide with northwesterly to northeasterly winds, or outgoing tide with southerly to easterly winds.

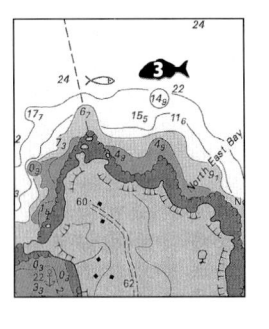

4 Woody Island

From the island north is a very kelpy, broken shoreline. Anchor so your berley runs along the shore, past Woody Island.

Ideal conditions Incoming tide with northwesterly to northerly winds or outgoing tide with westerly to southwesterly winds.

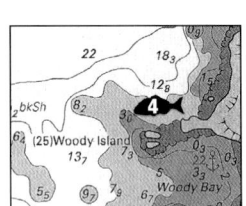

Winter

The summer spots often produce a good feed of fish in winter, too, so it is worth looking at them on the sounder before heading into shore. The best fishing is had by straylining close in; berley and groundbait are a must. It will often take an hour or so to bring the snapper on to the bite in the shallows.

1 Three Sisters

Straylining is best here in the evening. A lot of small, pan-size fish hole up in the area, so just take enough for a meal. The odd big fish also hangs around here, and I have been spooled more than once.

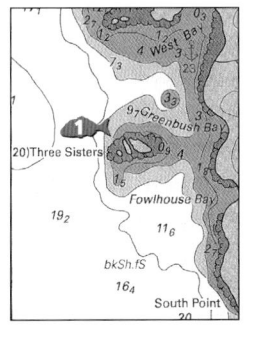

Ideal conditions Incoming tide with westerly to northwesterly winds (northern side), or outgoing tide with southwesterly to easterly winds (southern side).

2 Woody Island

There is a reef between the island and shore. Anchor in the gap on the north side, 50 m from shore. The tide will take your lines along and down past the shore, so cast uptide and walk the bait down the shoreline with the current.

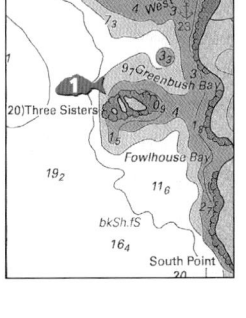

Ideal conditions Incoming tide with northerly winds.

3 Maori Garden Bay

A finger of reef runs out to the southeast, but the bay is fairly bouldery with lots of kelp so you may lose a bit of tackle. The end of the reef drops off to 10 m and, on an outgoing tide, you can fish back and take advantage of the fact that the berley drops down both sides of the reef. However, if the tide is strong you will find that you hang

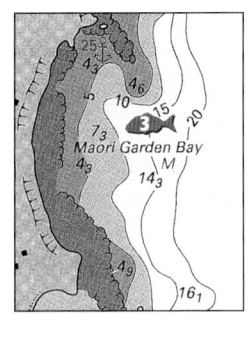

Maori Garden Bay

more out to sea; at these times it is better to move in, parallel to the end of the reef. You will not need sinkers at all, and be sure to cast a bait into the bay, too, as not all lazy fish live around the reef.

Ideal conditions Incoming tide with northerly to northeasterly winds (anchor on the north side of the finger so you fish down the length of it), or outgoing tide with southerly to southwesterly winds.

4 The Northern End

The shoreline at the very northern end of Rakino curves slightly inwards as it heads west and contains a reef that curves out to the north. Anchor so that the stern of the boat is to the middle of the reef and within casting distance of the kelp.

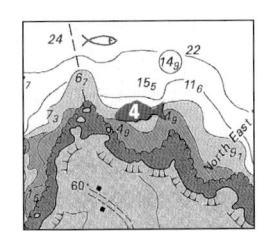

Ideal conditions Incoming tide with northwesterly to northerly winds.

Area ⑨ The Noises and Ahaaha Rocks

Habitat

Care needs to be taken in this area as it is strewn with semi-submerged rocks and reefs. In deeper water the bottom consists of mud, broken shell and sand, and there is an abundance of shellfish, crabs and worms — an ideal food source for snapper. The reefs and rocks also feature lots of kelp, which hold more delights for the snapper, including kina, mussels and limpets. Baitfish such as slimy mackerel, sprats, koheru and piper are often found here in big numbers, and the area is therefore also good for targeting kingfish and John Dory. Although the Noises and Ahaahas come under enormous pressure from the hordes of people who fish here, the rocks, reef structures and islands are spread over a big area. Despite its popularity, this is one of my favourite areas as it has so many good fishing spots close together.

The Noises

Caution: not to be used for navigation.

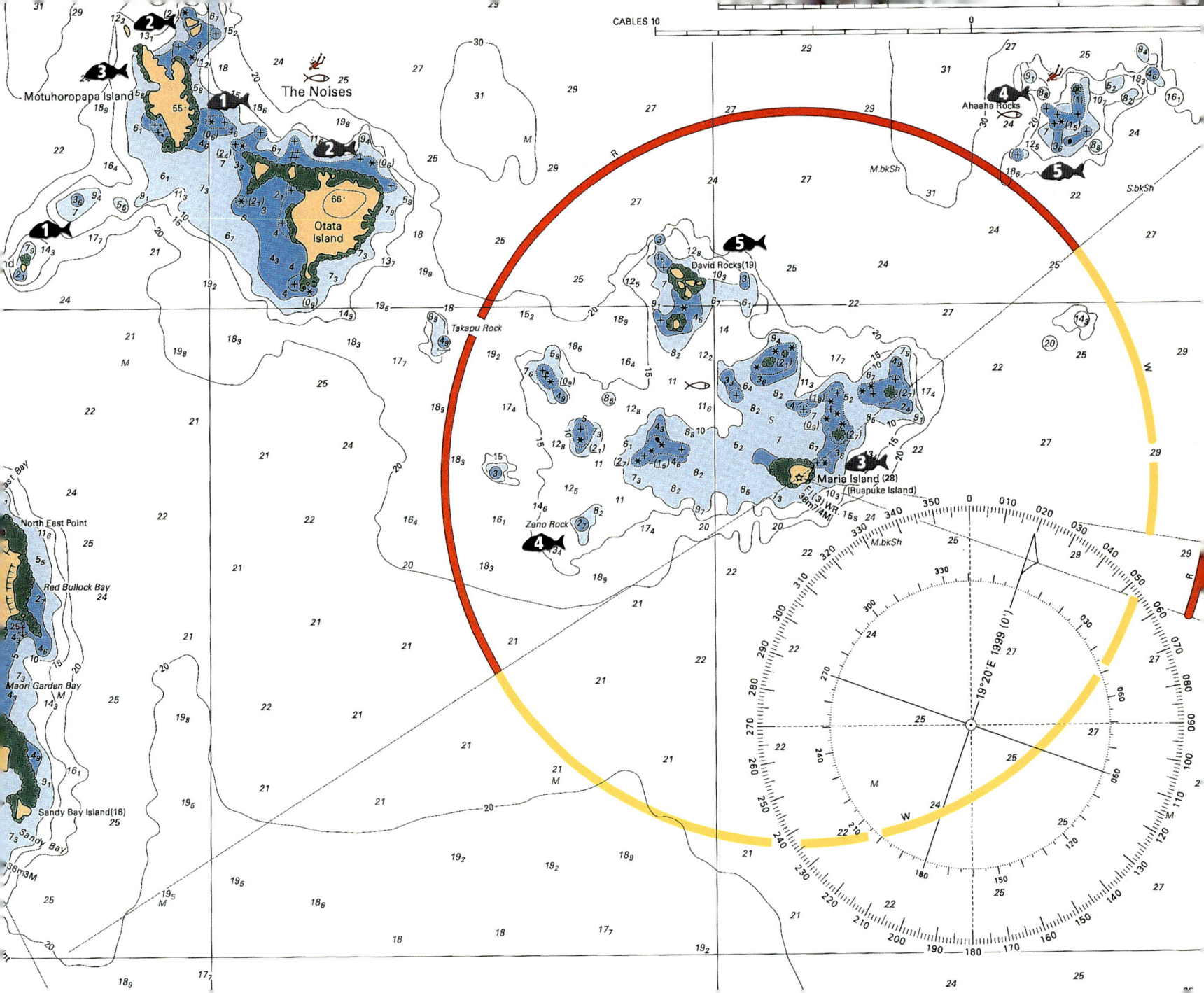

Summer

Often as early as September, a run of big buck (male) snapper comes into this area as a sort of advance party for the females. They generally hang around in the Ahaahas area before mixing with the later-arriving school fish. Once the spawning snapper arrive en masse, you could be excused if, at times, you thought your sounder was playing up. A big mass of snapper shows up as red on a colour sounder, and this will often be so solid that it looks like a reef. In time, these masses of school fish break up and spread out over a wide area looking for food. I find it best to head north first — I start looking in the 31-m hole north of Otata Island and then zigzag back and forth towards David Rocks. If you see current lines, follow them, but do so at low speed to check if the snapper are feeding there. There is an enormous amount to be learned by looking at the sounder and noting the size and movements of the snapper schools in summer.

1 The Haystack (Orarapa Island)

Take a line from the Haystack to the gap between the two big Noises islands. Note the way the bottom rises from 17 m to 3.6 m and then drops off again. Close by are two pinnacles of 6.7 m and 5.5 m — the best way to find them is to zigzag back and forth as you get close to the target area. You will find the snapper hanging on the drop-off in the current, so fish back to them rather than trying to fish on top of the pinnacles.

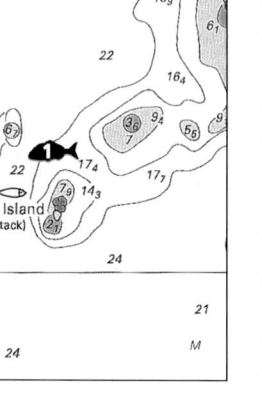

Ideal conditions Incoming tide with northwesterly to westerly winds, or outgoing tide with southwesterly to westerly winds.

2 Motuhoropapa Island

There are two large exposed rocks on the northern end of the island, with further sunken rocks beyond. Strayline around these areas on either tidal flow.

Ideal conditions Incoming tide with northerly to easterly winds, or outgoing tide with westerly to southerly winds.

3 Motuhoropapa Drop-off

Note the finger of deeper water to the west. A lot of fish move through here, and I find most at the point where the bottom drops from 13.4 m to 24 m.

Ideal conditions Incoming tide with northwesterly to northerly winds, or outgoing tide with southwesterly to southeasterly winds.

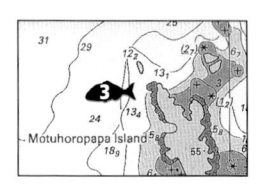

4 Zeno Rock

Zeno Rock comes up to 2.7 m and a reef extends to the northeast before the bottom drops to 8.2 m. Anchor back in 10–12 m of water and strayline into the reef structure. This spot can be dynamite on an incoming tide at dusk.

Ideal conditions Incoming tide with northwesterly to northeasterly winds (northern side of the rock), or outgoing tide with southwesterly to easterly winds (southeastern side of the rock).

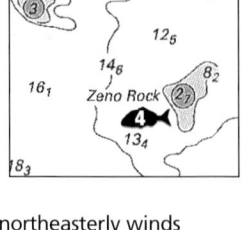

5 David Rocks

With the sounder set on zoom, take a look at the bottom between the two 3-m marks on the northern side of David Rocks. Snapper often hold here on the edge of the drop-off in 15–18 m. They can also often be found around the 12-m mark on the southern side.

Ideal conditions Incoming tide with northerly to northeasterly winds (northern side), or in westerly to southwesterly winds (southern side).

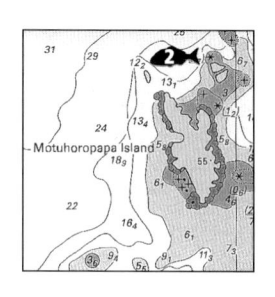

Winter

Many of the summer spots still hold fish right through the winter, and the best way to fish them is by straylining with lots of berley and groundbait. In winter, my game plan is to fish one spot right through a tidal phase, which I have found to be more productive than moving about (see 'Straylining', page 26). Arrive early and spend time looking at the bottom on the sounder to build up a good knowledge of the whole area. Try new spots occasionally as there are plenty here waiting to be discovered and this is a great way to increase your local knowledge. Note that in the case of the Ahaahas, no one spot is that much better than any other as one side or end will fish one day but not the next. Spend time in the area trying different spots, and build up your own database and history in your mind.

1 Ratty's Rock

At the southeastern end of the island is a submerged rock and one that is awash. In a runabout, anchor between, and slightly to the north of, the rock that is awash and the island. Strayline back down the shoreline. (This is not the place for launches!)

Ideal conditions Incoming tide with winds from the northwest to northeast.

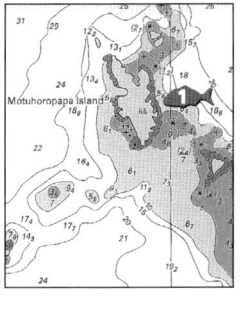

2 Otata Island

There is a rock that is awash at the northeastern end of the island and a foul area here (down to 9 m before it drops off) that runs north. I have always found that the western side of this structure fishes best.

Ideal conditions Incoming tide with northeasterly to northerly winds.

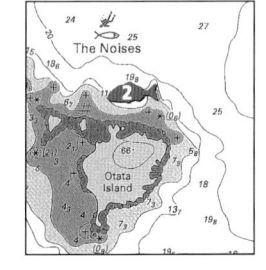

3 Maria Island

Extending north from the island is an extensive area of exposed and submerged structures. The whole area is very fishable and best on an incoming tide with northerly quarter winds. Let the boat settle before you start to fish as, in some tides, you will not be

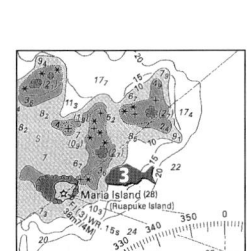

lying the way you would expect. Berley, groundbait and patience have always produced fish here for me.

Ideal conditions Incoming tide with north-northwesterly to northeasterly winds.

4 The Ahaahas (Northern Side)

On the northern side of the Ahaahas the bottom drops off steeply from the main reef structure and there are pinnacles rising to 9 m. The key to this area is to have the stern of the boat facing square to the structure so that your baits float back down the berley trail.

Ideal conditions Incoming tide with northerly to easterly winds.

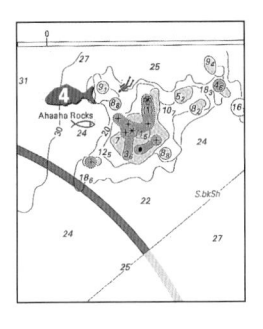

5 The Ahaahas (Southern Side)

Again, it is important here how the boat lies to the wind and tide. The same rules apply: be square on so that both berley and baits flow back into the structure.

Ideal conditions Outgoing tide with southwesterly to southeasterly winds.

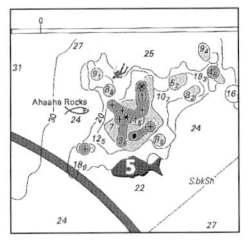

Area  Owhanake to Te Whau Point

Habitat

Waiheke's northern coast, from Owhanake to Te Whau Point, is an often overlooked stretch of shoreline with a lot of fishing potential. When the wind is blowing strong from the south, the high cliffs here funnel it down the valleys and create back eddies that allow you to lie parallel to the shore. Local knowledge is always a bonus, and this is a great place to hone your skills and add to your personal database. Between Hakaimango and Thompsons points there are many small bays with exposed rocky islets and reefs. In the bigger bays and further offshore, the bottom consists largely of sand and broken shell with a few pieces of low foul. There is a good food supply here for snapper, with baitfish all year round and crabs, worms and shellfish out on the sand. In the very kelp-covered rocky reefs and islets there are also limpets, snails and shellfish.

Thompsons Point

Caution: not to be used for navigation.

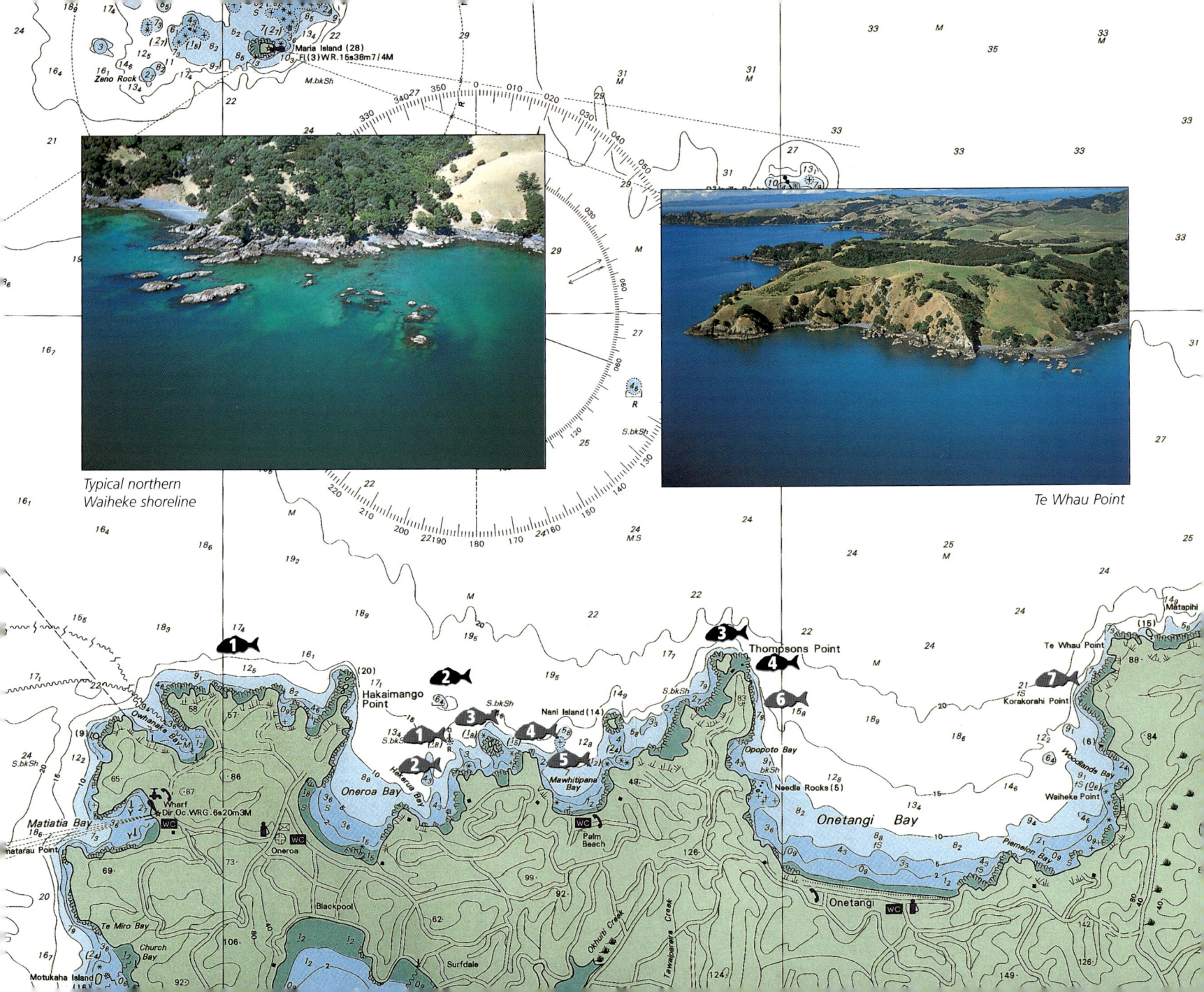

Typical northern
Waiheke shoreline

Te Whau Point

Summer

There are often big work-ups off the headlands or in the open water between Oneroa and Onetangi as the tidal flow brings nutrients to the surface, attracting baitfish. These in turn attract kahawai, kingfish and birds, and the snapper, ever alert to a free feed, gorge on the scraps below. Jigging or drift fishing with baited flasher or ledger rigs can result in a very full fish bin in a very short time. On calm days, try using a bait net on one of the sandy beaches — it's great fun for the whole family and a fresh bait used right on dusk can result in a nice big moocher. When a strong wind is blowing against the tide this whole area can be an uncomfortable place to fish. Setting a longline here at such times can be a great back-up while you fish in a more sheltered spot.

1 Owhanake to Hakaimango Point

There is a reasonably strong tidal flow in this area, and I prefer to zigzag slowly from the 10-m line out to about 18 m with the sounder set on zoom, looking for fish marks. Before anchoring, test any sign with a baited flasher rig as it is easy to mistake the dense schools of baitfish for snapper.

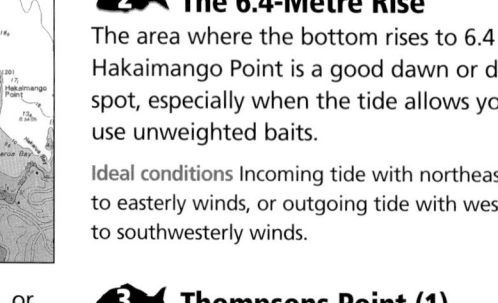

Ideal conditions Incoming tide with northeasterly to easterly winds, or outgoing tide with northwesterly to southwesterly winds.

2 The 6.4-Metre Rise

The area where the bottom rises to 6.4 m off Hakaimango Point is a good dawn or dusk spot, especially when the tide allows you to use unweighted baits.

Ideal conditions Incoming tide with northeasterly to easterly winds, or outgoing tide with westerly to southwesterly winds.

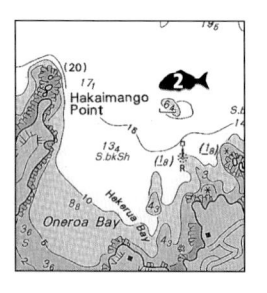

3 Thompsons Point (1)

Anchor in 12 m so that the stern of the boat is facing the islet off the point. Use a weighted berley bag and lots of groundbait.

Ideal conditions Outgoing tide with westerly to southwesterly winds.

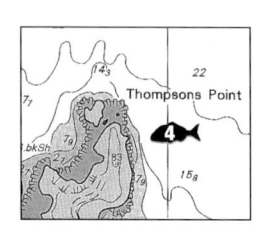

4 Thompsons Point (2)

Anchor to the east of the headland so your stern is facing the big guts or channels. Strayline big baits back into the kelp.

Ideal conditions Incoming tide with north to easterly winds.

Hakaimango Point

Winter

The kelpy shoreline and numerous rocks and reefs along this stretch provide a good home for resident snapper during the winter. The key is always to use as much knowledge as you have to choose one spot along the rocky shoreline and then stick with it through the whole tide, straylining with lots of berley and groundbait. Bigger snapper can be caught on a butterflied bait, set well back with no drag so the cautious fish does not feel any resistance.

➊◄ The Northern Bays

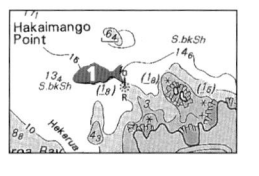

To the east of Oneroa are Hekerua, Sandy and Enclosure bays, all of which offer a number of good straylining spots.

Ideal conditions Incoming tide with northerly to northeasterly winds, or outgoing tide with southwesterly to westerly winds.

➋◄ The Rises

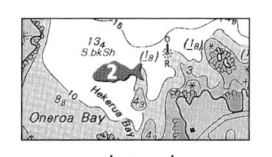

There is a series of rises (4.3 m, 4.6 m, 4.3 m, 4.9 m and 8.2 m) indicated on the chart between Hekerua and Sandy bays. Choose the spot that is best suited to the wind, lay down a good steady berley trail and strayline with unweighted baits.

Ideal conditions Incoming tide with northerly to northeasterly winds, or outgoing tide with southwesterly to southerly winds.

➌◄ Enclosure Bay Rock (Marked)

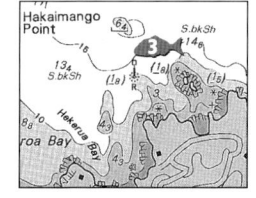

The rock at the entrance to the bay is often a good place to use unweighted baits at dawn or dusk.

Ideal conditions Incoming tide with northerly to northeasterly winds (northern side), or outgoing tide with westerly to southwesterly winds (southern side).

➍◄ Enclosure Bay Islets

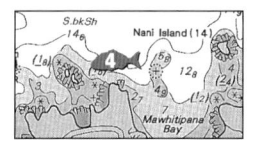

There is good fishing on the northern side of the reef structure that runs between these islets and the shore.

Ideal conditions Incoming tide with northerly to northeasterly winds.

➎◄ Mawhitipana Bay

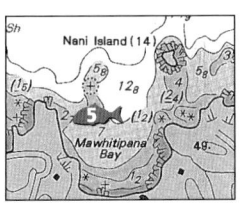

There is an 11-m hole here with a rock that is awash to its north. When the southerly is strong it can swirl off the land, making for some frustrating fishing, although the results can be worthwhile.

Ideal conditions Incoming tide with northeasterly to easterly winds, or outgoing tide with westerly to southwesterly winds.

➏◄ Thompsons Point

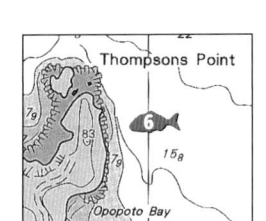

Although most of the boats in this area seem to fish right on the end of the point, I have had better catches halfway down towards Opopoto Bay using unweighted baits cast back to the kelp line. I have also experienced some massive bust-offs at dusk after berleying for hours, so it's an exciting place to fish.

Ideal conditions Incoming tide with northerly to easterly winds, or outgoing tide with southerly to southeasterly winds.

➐◄ Korakorahi Point to Te Whau Point

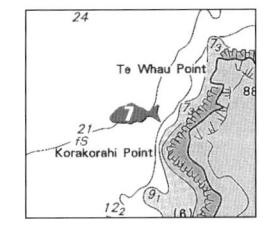

Although there is little to see on either the chart or the sounder, I have experienced some stunning fishing here. Look for small areas of rubble combined with fish marks, and use small sinkers to cast well back from the boat.

Ideal conditions Outgoing tide with southwesterly winds.

Area  Te Whau Point to Thumb Point

Habitat

This is an interesting area to fish as both the bottom and the environment vary enormously and there are a number of good fishing spots very close to one another. The shoreline, where it is not sandy, features a lot of kelp and there is a big population of limpets, snails and kina. The sand is home to good numbers of crab and shellfish, and a lot of baitfish stay in the area all year. Gannets can often be seen feeding as nutrients and baitfish are brought close to the surface by the strong tidal flow. There is great fishing here after a strong storm from the north, as the bottom gets churned up and a smorgasbord of food is exposed for the snapper to feed on.

Broken shoreline northeast of Owhiti Bay

Caution: not to be used for navigation.

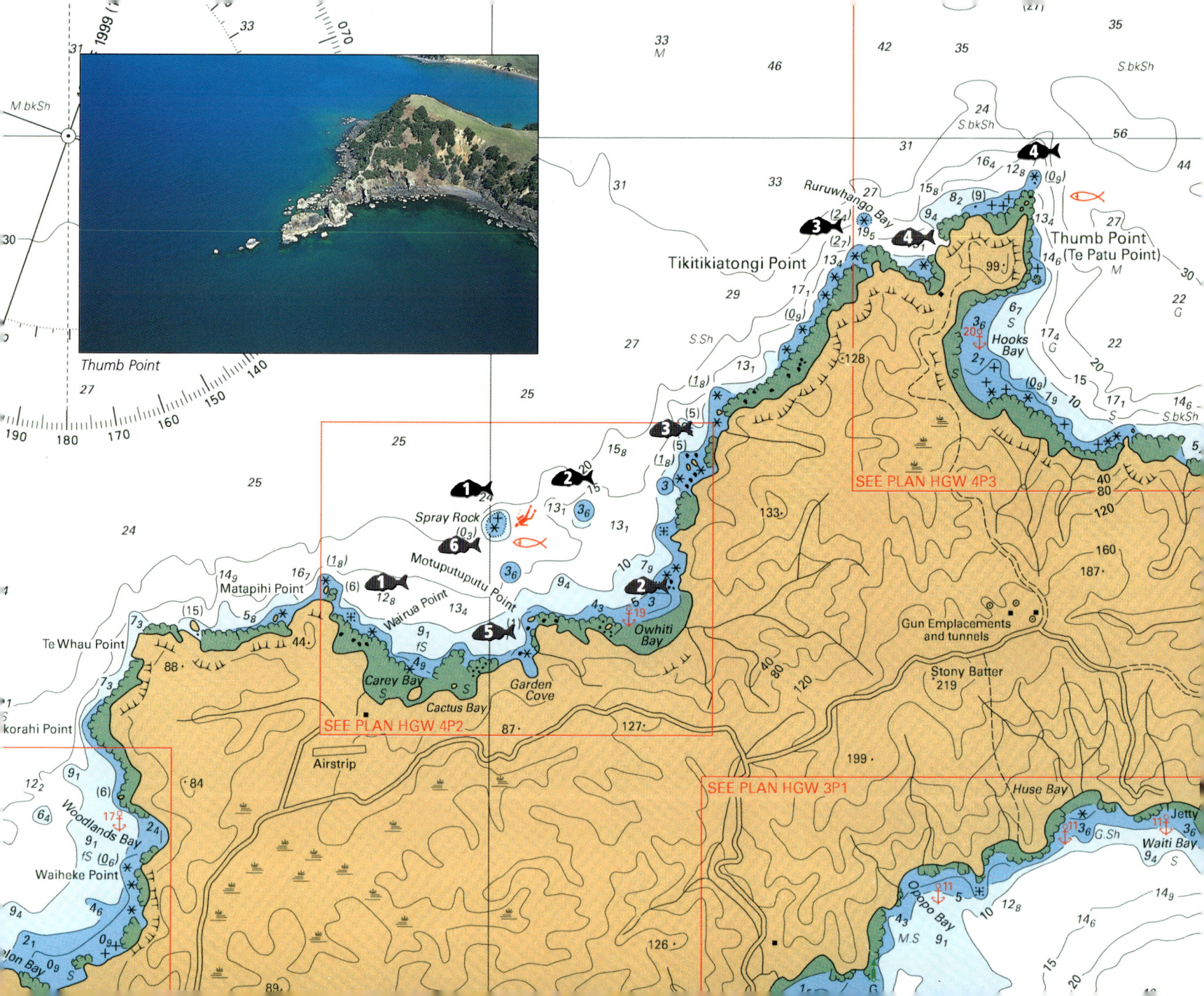

Summer

Drift fishing and jigging out on the open sand using ledger and flasher rigs can be productive, but the wind and tide must be running in the same direction. Calmer weather is best as, if the wind is over 15 knots and the tide run is strong, conditions can become a bit sloppy.

1 Spray Rock

I see a lot of boats that make the mistake of anchoring on (not wise!) or too close to Spray Rock. It is far better to note the wind and tide directions and then anchor so that you can fish back up to the rock.

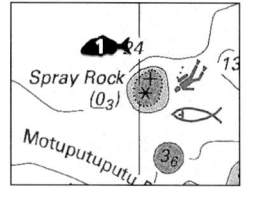

Ideal conditions Incoming tide with northerly through to easterly winds, or outgoing tide with westerly to southerly winds.

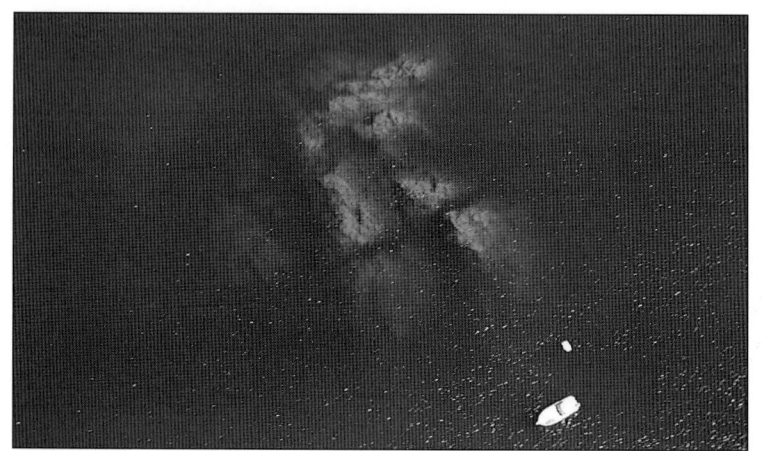

Spray Rock

2 The Pinnacle

Almost due east from Spray Rock is a pinnacle of rock standing on its own. This rock can really fire with good-size fish on the change of light, particularly at dusk.

Ideal conditions Incoming tide with northerly to easterly winds, or outgoing tide with southwesterly to southerly winds.

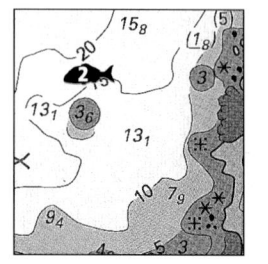

3 Tikitikiatongi Point to Thumb Point

Keeping a careful watch on the sounder, work a zigzag pattern out from the shore until you come across some broken foul, which (hopefully!) is covered in fish. Before anchoring, try a flasher rig as big schools of maomao can often be misinterpreted as snapper.

Ideal conditions Incoming tide with northerly to northeasterly winds, or outgoing tide with southwesterly to southerly winds.

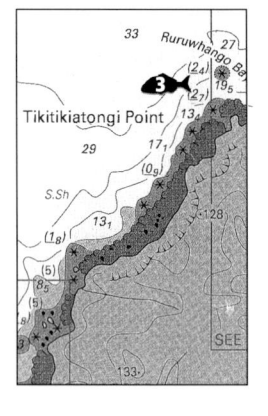

4 Thumb Point

Approach the headland from the west and note the way the bottom rises and falls away in a series of big valleys. Put the sounder on maximum zoom and slowly work from the bottom of a valley up to the top. Again, calm conditions when the wind and tide are running together are best, as a fierce tidal run and an opposing wind can make the sea resemble a washing machine. Flasher and ledger rigs work particularly well here.

Ideal conditions Incoming tide with northwesterly to easterly winds, or outgoing tide with westerly to southerly winds.

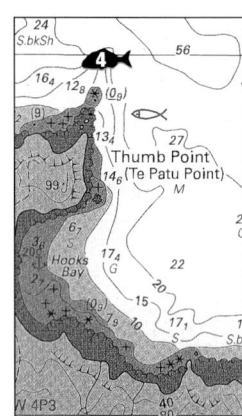

Winter

The summer spots are also worth looking at during winter, although consistently there seem to be more fish in the shallows. When straylining these shallows remember that they hold an abundance of natural food, so be sure to use plenty of berley and groundbait to bring the fish to your baits and on the bite.

1 Carey Bay

The shoreline from Carey Bay out to the headland provides good fishing for pan-size snapper. Strayline back into the kelpy shoreline.

Ideal conditions Incoming tide with northerly to easterly winds.

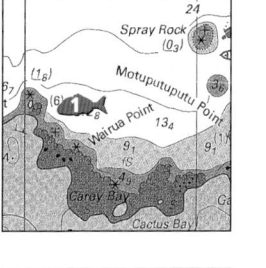

2 Owhiti Bay

When anchored in this bay for the night I have always caught pan-size snapper by straylining at dawn and dusk.

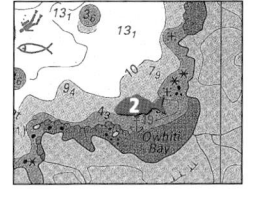

3 Owhiti Bay to Thumb Point

Close to shore from the western end of Owhiti right along to Thumb Point is ideal straylining habitat. The key to targeting winter snapper here is to ensure the wind and tide are running in the same direction and to position the boat so that a bait can easily be cast close to the rocks. The berley trail will move a long way down the shoreline over the run of a tide, so be sure to stick with it even if you don't get bites at first — the fish will come on.

Ideal conditions Incoming tide with northerly to northeasterly winds, or outgoing tide with southwesterly to southerly winds.

4 Ruruwhango Bay

This bay comes under heavy fishing pressure but it can produce some big fish after a northerly storm has passed and really stirred up the bottom.

Ideal conditions Incoming tide north to northeast winds or outgoing tide west to southwest winds.

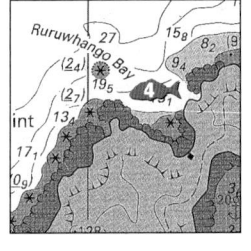

5 Garden Cove

To the west of the entrance the bottom undulates and is fairly featureless, but often fishes very well just on dusk.

Ideal conditions Incoming tide east to northeast winds or outgoing tide west to northwest winds.

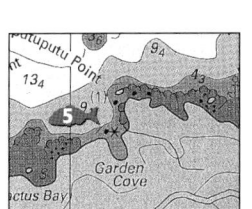

6 Wairua Point to Spray Rock

Drift fishing from Wairua Point to Spray Rock can be all on, or all off, but it is the area that can put a meal on the table when all other spots fail. I have found the best results have been in light winds with the boat drifting slowly.

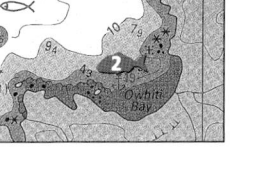

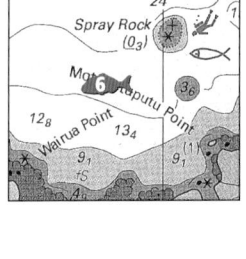

Area 12 **Thumb Point** to **Kauri Point** (Including Gannet Rock)

Habitat

If you take a line from Thumb Point out to Gannet Rock then down to the 14-m pinnacle northeast of Kauri Point, you will find an area with a bottom that is mainly sandy mud with a lot of broken shell and the odd bit of low foul. The water in this area is at depths of between 30 m and over 50 m, and the strong tidal movement brings up the nutrients on which the masses of baitfish feed. The snapper fishing is consistent year round, with good pan-size fish easily caught; at times, schools of 5–6-kg snapper also hold in the area. As the tidal flow is strong here, it can be quite rough if the wind is blowing against it at over 15 knots, but there are a lot of fishing options. As you would expect in an area with lots of baitfish, plenty of kahawai and kingfish also stay here. Hooks Bay is a good place year round to use a bait net for sprats and piper.

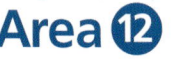

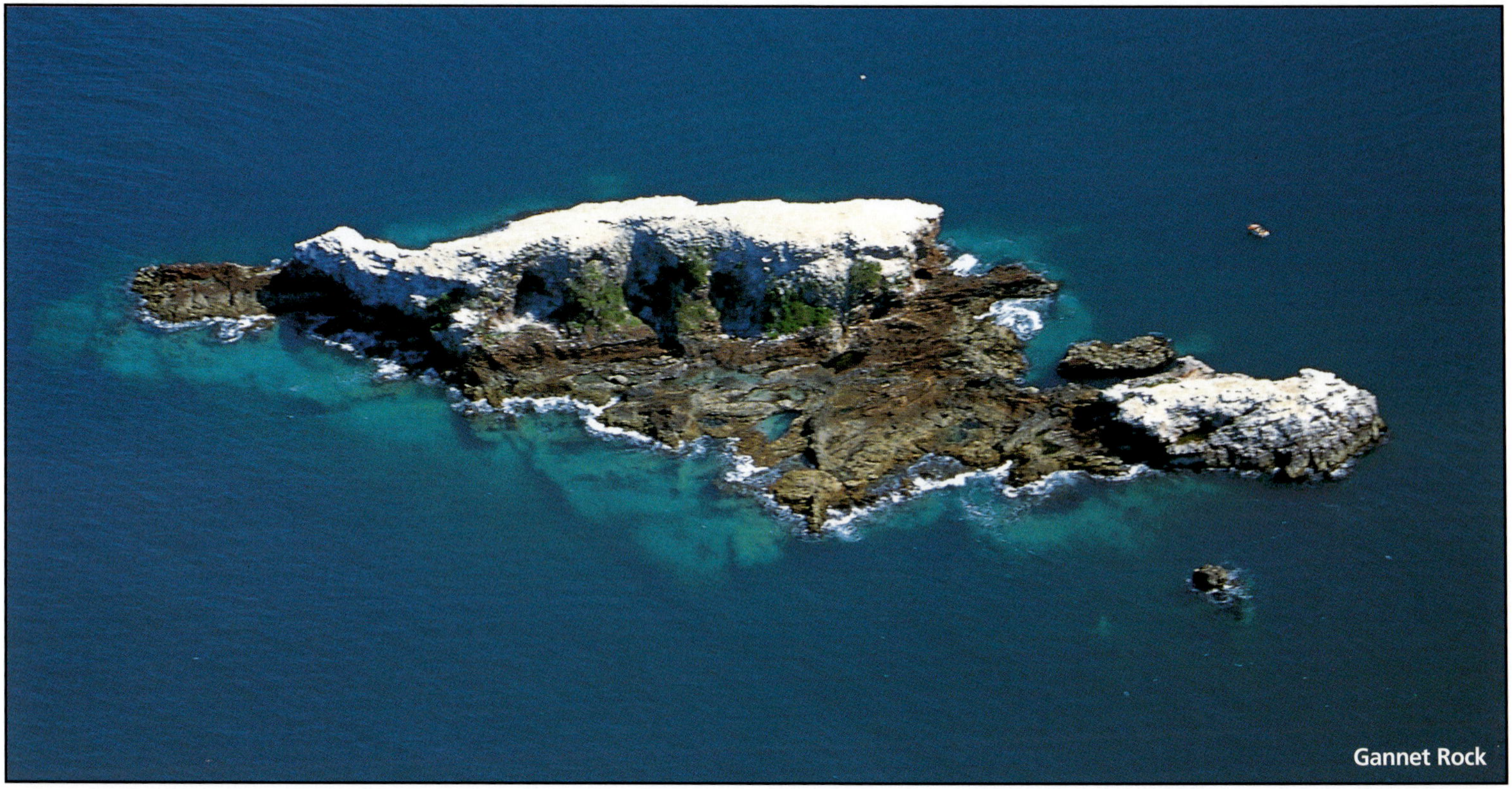

Gannet Rock

Caution: not to be used for navigation.

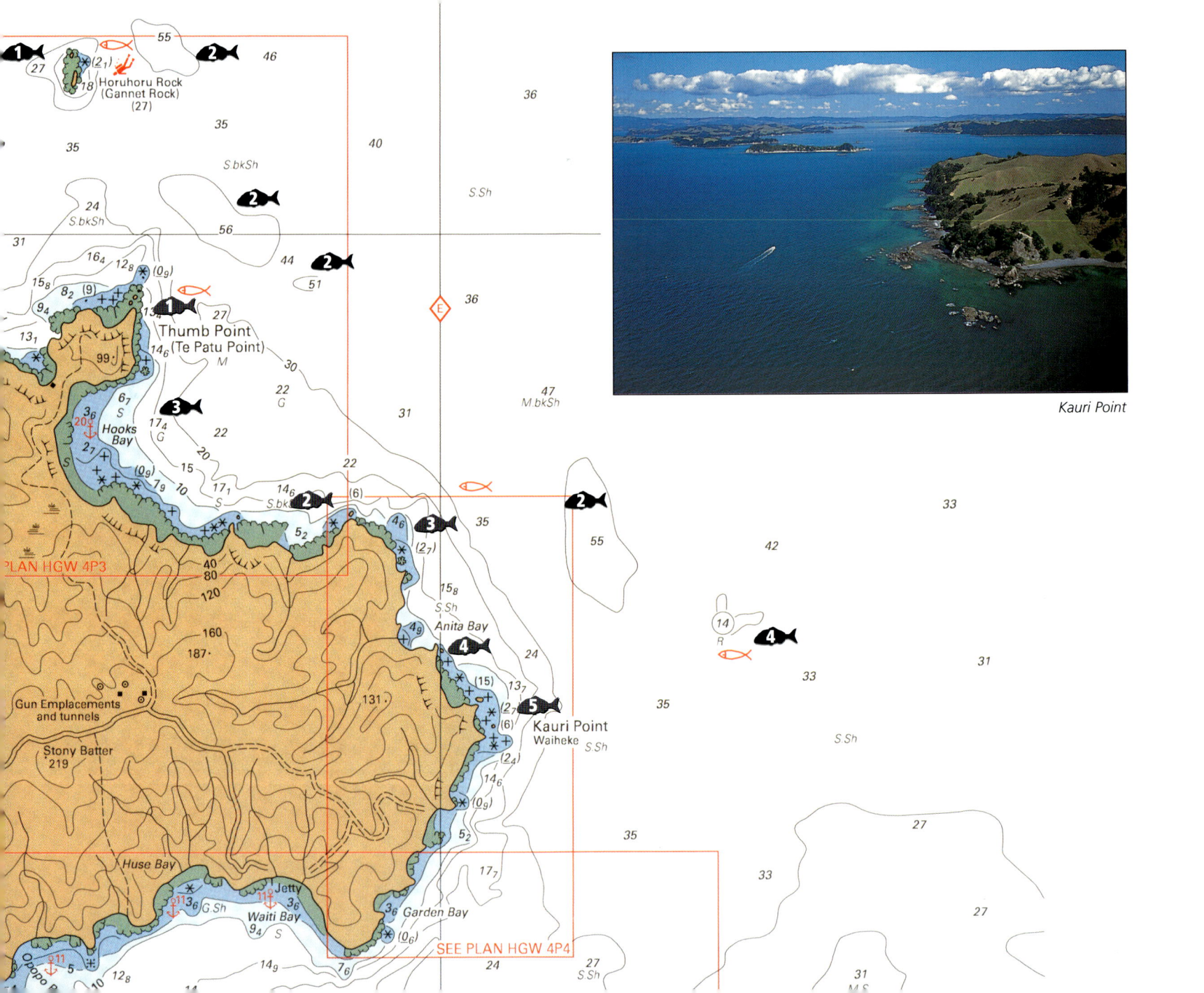

55

① 27 | **(2₁)** | **② 46**

Horuhoru Rock
(Gannet Rock)
(27)

18

36

35

S.bkSh

35   40   **S.Sh**

24
S.bkSh   **② 56**

31

16₄ 12₈ (0₉)

15₈ 8₂ (9)

9₄

13₁

① 13₄ 27

Thumb Point
(Te Patu Point)
14₆ : 99 : M   30   44 **②** 51

36

E

22
G

31

47
M.bkSh

67
S

③ 17₄
G   22

3₆
⚓
20⚓

Hooks
Bay   20   15

(0₉) 7₉ 10   17₁
S   14₆
S.bks   **② (6)**   35   **② 55**

5₂   4₆
③ (2₇)

42

33

PLAN HGW 4P3   40
80

120

15₈
S.Sh

4₉   **Anita Bay**   24

14
R   **④**

160
187·

④   (15)   13₇
(2₇)
(6)   **⑤**   27

33

31

Gun Emplacements
and tunnels   131·   (2₄)   **Kauri Point**
Waiheke   S.Sh

35   S.Sh

Stony Batter
· 219   14₆
(0₉)

5₂

219

Huse Bay   17₇

35

33

⚓13₆
G.Sh   Jetty 3₆
11⚓   3₆   Garden Bay
Waiti Bay   (0₆)
9₄ S

27
S.Sh

27

⚓11   5
Opooo P.   12₈   14₉   7₆   **SEE PLAN HGW 4P4**   24

31
M.S

Kauri Point

Summer

The Firth of Thames (see page 102) is a big spawning area for snapper over the summer months and the school fish arrive around late September/early October. Initially, they largely stay out in deeper water before moving inshore around December. When the snapper are spawning (between November and January) they can be very difficult to catch, and although the sounder may show lots of fish signs nothing will actually take a bait. At times like this I find there are three options:

• **Jigging** The jigs seem to get hit out of aggression rather than as food.

• **Drift fishing** Baited flasher rigs or ledger rigs often get better results when drifting rather than at anchor.

• **Fishing fast-flowing water** The one thing that does make fish more likely to hit baits is fast-flowing water, so look for areas of fast tidal flow. Anchor and try using both a ledger rig and a running rig with a 1.5–2-m trace.

① Gannet Rock

As Gannet Rock is actually quite small, it is worth spending time steaming around the area at low speed with the sounder set on zoom. This is one place where the fishing can be quiet one moment and then suddenly fire up with good-sized fish. To the western side of the rock the bottom contours out at 27 m on the chart. Anchor at 27 m and fish back down the drop-off.

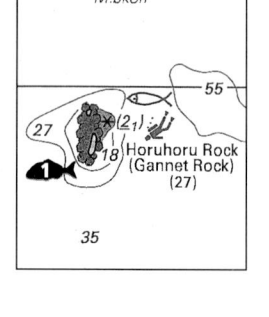

Ideal conditions Incoming tide with northeasterly to northwesterly winds.

② The Deep Holes

Not far offshore from Hooks Bay are four deep holes (55 m, 56 m, 51 m and 53 m), clearly visible on the chart. It is very rare for there to be no fish sign on the sounder over these holes, and this is an ideal area to jig and drift fish with baited flasher and ledger rigs. You will need 4–6-oz sinkers in order to

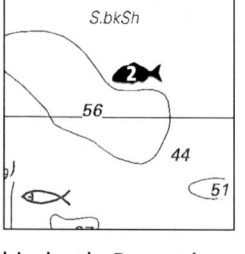

keep in touch with your baits when drifting in this depth. Do not just drift through the middle of the holes as fish will often be sitting on the edges or ends of the banks.

③ Hooks Bay

Hooks Bay is often overlooked because of its wide-open, flat, sandy bottom. When the wind is too strong to fish deep water comfortably, I come into the bay until the sounder reads 10 m and then drift fish back out again. More often than not, once I get over the 17-m contour the fish become more spaced out and so I head back in again.

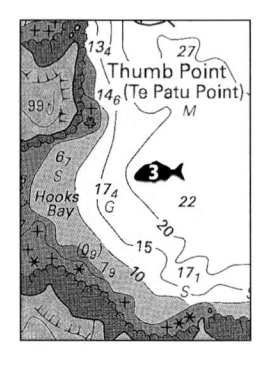

Ideal conditions Westerly to southeasterly winds.

④ 14-Metre Pinnacle

Approximately 1 mile north-northeast of Kauri Point is a pinnacle (complete with a bit of reef extending north and northeast of the rock) rising to 14 m. At times around October and late April, some schools of snapper up to 5–6 kg hold here and can be attracted with big butterflied baits (see photograph page 19). Always fish when the wind and tide are running in the same direction — unless you enjoy rolling about.

Ideal conditions Incoming tide with northwesterly to northeasterly winds, or outgoing tide with southwesterly to southeasterly winds.

Winter

The summer spots will generally still fish reasonably well in winter but, if the winds are 15 knots or over, I prefer to target the snapper close to shore. The rocky shoreline features lots of kelp, with good populations of kina, mussels, limpets and snails. As the wind can funnel down the high cliffs and valleys, side-anchoring the boat will often ensure that you lay with the tide, thereby making it easier to strayline properly.

🐟 Thumb Point

At the end of the headland are a few exposed rocks that extend out from the shore. With the strong tidal flow in the area, this spot makes for some excellent fishing, particularly at dusk. Anchor approximately 20 m from the shore, slightly back from the end of the point.

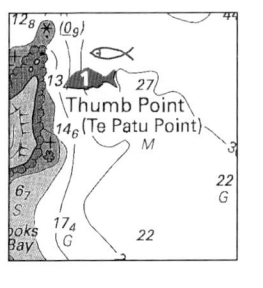

Ideal conditions Outgoing tide with southerly to easterly winds.

🐟 Hooks Bay (1)

The southern shoreline of Hooks Bay, from the middle of the bay out to the exposed rock at the headland, is very rocky and fishes well in winter. If the wind and tidal flow are right you can anchor as close as 10 m offshore and get a berley trail running right down into the kelpy rocks. Fresh piper bait has often proven to be irresistible, even to the most shy of snapper.

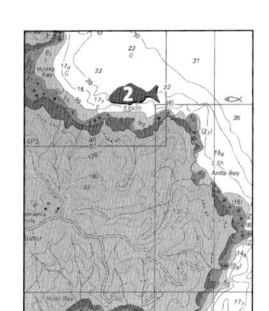

Ideal conditions Incoming tide with westerly to northerly winds.

🐟 Hooks Bay (2)

Just around and out from the southern end of Hooks Bay is a reef structure that comes up to 4–6 m. However, anchoring on top of the reef seldom produces fish of any size. Instead, anchor back from the reef in approximately 14–18 m and fish back up into it. Berley just

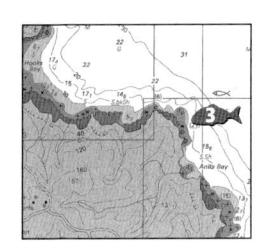

off the bottom and use groundbait (see 'Berley and Groundbait', page 32), particularly just at dusk.

Ideal conditions Incoming tide with northwesterly to northeasterly winds (fish from the northern side), or outgoing tide with southwesterly to southeasterly winds (fish from the southern side).

🐟 Anita Bay

The southern end of this bay curves back out to the north and is only fishable on an incoming tide with a northerly wind. I have caught nice fish, even on a bright sunny day, by creating a good berley trail (and using groundbait) and straylining unweighted baits back into the rocky shore.

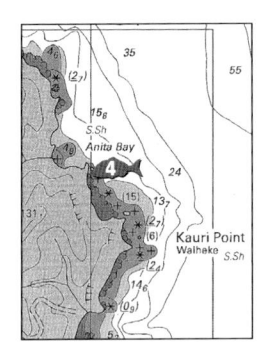

Ideal conditions Incoming tide with a northerly wind.

🐟 Kauri Point

There are a lot of submerged and exposed rocks around the headland and great care needs to be taken when fishing close in to shore. The northern side of Kauri Point is by far the best and can only be fished on the incoming tide. A lot of berley and groundbait are needed as the tide will take it well round the headland, in time bringing snapper from up to a mile or so away. Cast a pattern of baits from close along the shore back to the open water (see 'Straylining', page 26).

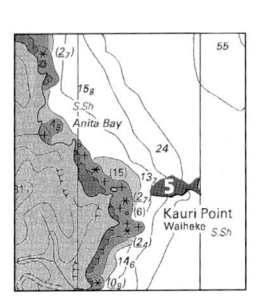

Ideal conditions Incoming tide with north-northwesterly to northerly winds.

Area 13 Kauri Point to Ruthe Passage

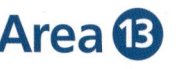

Habitat

Between Kauri Point and the southern end of Ruthe Passage on Ponui Island are Pakatoa and Rotoroa islands, and 'inside' of these is the Waiheke Channel. This channel is shallower at the Ponui end (over 14 m), dropping down to as much as 46 m off Pakatoa. As the tide changes, a huge amount of water from the Tamaki Strait flows through here, bringing nutrients that feed the resident baitfish — and the crabs and shellfish that inhabit the largely muddy and sandy bottom. A lot of bays have both mud and rock oysters, mussels and limpets, and snails and crabs living among the seaweed. This type of bottom offers a food source for the snapper that come in to spawn. Many of the muddy bays are home to flounder and mullet, and the area is often thick with small kahawai.

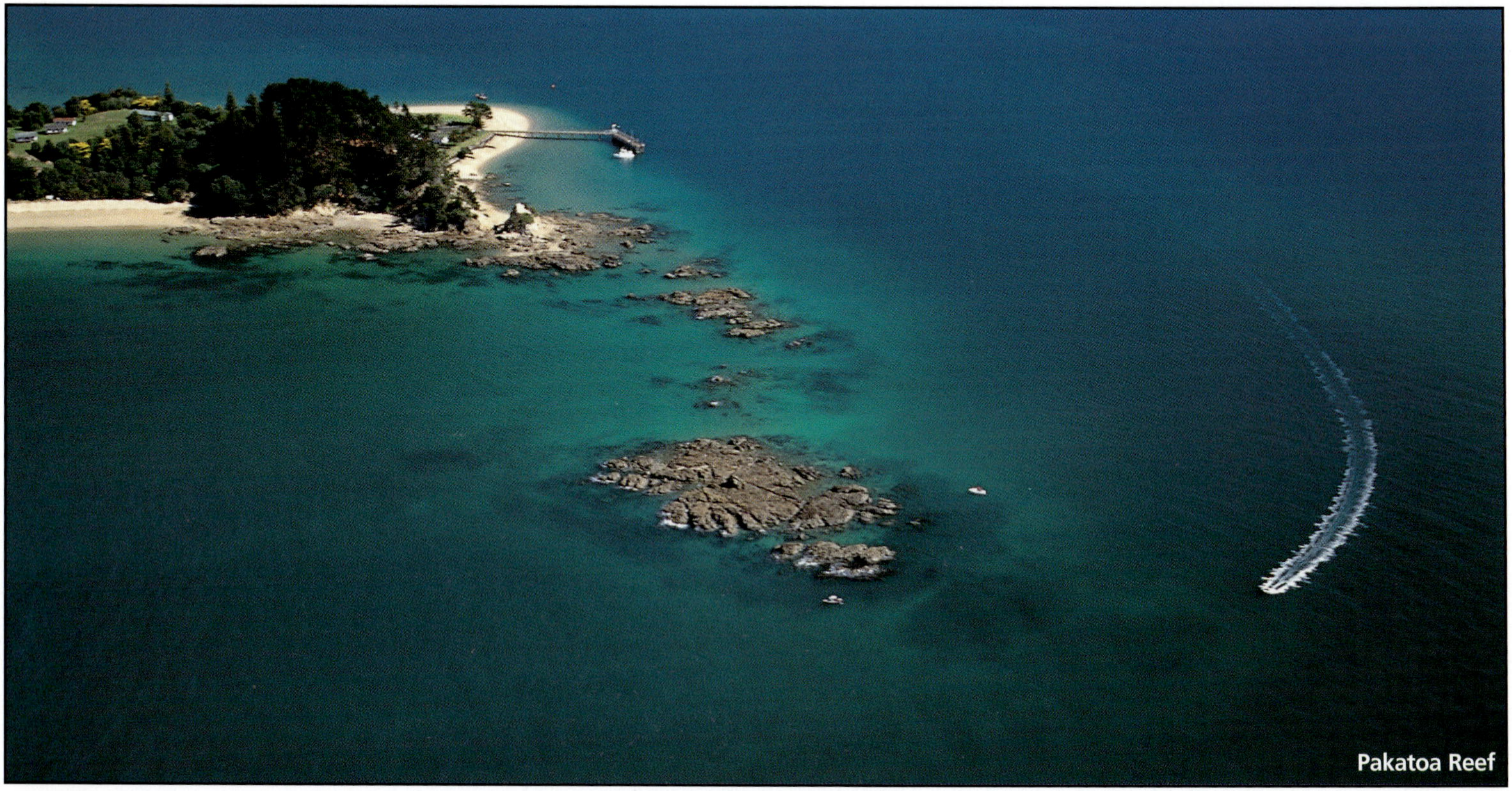

Pakatoa Reef

Caution: not to be used for navigation.

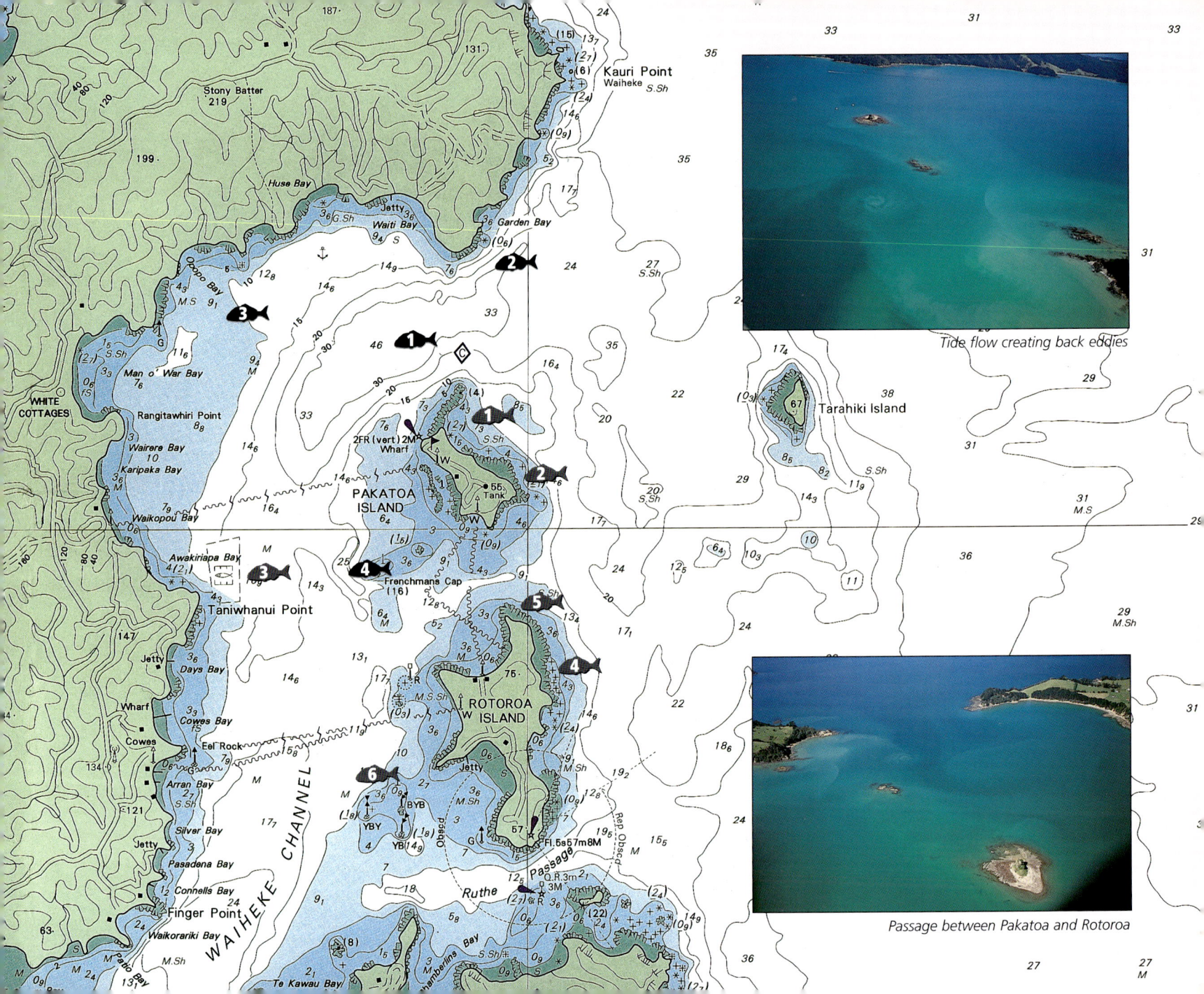

Tide flow creating back eddies

Passage between Pakatoa and Rotoroa

Summer

From November or December the school fish start to work their way into this area. They often stay largely in the stretch from Frenchmans Cap to Kauri Point, where there is good tidal flow and a lot of natural food. There are few snapper close in around the shoreline of the islands as most of the resident population move out to join the spawning school fish. The sounder often shows what appears to be snapper on the bottom. However, when you zoom in, you'll see fish marks that spike up 2–3 m off the bottom; these are usually schools of baitfish. Drop down a baited flasher rig anyway, as there are often snapper among them.

❶ The Finger (1)

On the chart, note a finger of deep water running parallel to both Waiheke and Pakatoa islands. The southern end is 46 m deep, rising to 33 m at the northern end. Drift fishing with baited flashers and ledger rigs is an effective way of covering this area (there are often more fish on the edges of the channel than in the middle).

Ideal conditions Incoming tide with northerly to northeasterly winds, or outgoing tide with southwesterly to southerly winds.

❷ The Finger (2)

On an outgoing tide, a lot of snapper hold in the area where the bottom rises at the northern end of this narrow finger (use the sounder to find the exact spot). They usually stay on the end of the rise but not on the top. The tidal flow is very strong so you may need up to 8 oz of weight to stay on the bottom. Squid and mullet are the best baits as they hang on better in the deep than do soft baits.

Ideal conditions Outgoing tide with southwesterly to southeasterly winds.

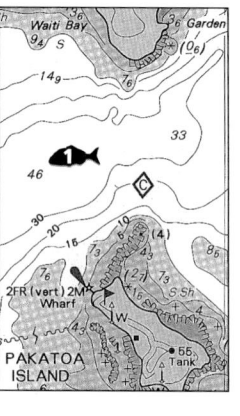

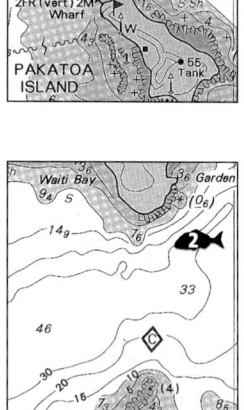

❸ Man o' War Bay to Waiti Bay

In late summer snapper move into this area to feed. Birds can often be seen working in this area, and jigging and drift fishing will produce decent pan-size snapper. This is also an ideal place to set a longline as the bottom (in 10–15 m of water) is clean of any foul.

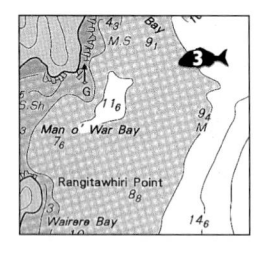

❹ Frenchmans Cap

Just slightly north of the island the bottom shelves down quite rapidly, and this drop-off consistently produces pan-size snapper. Fish back into the drop-off using a running rig with a 1–2-m trace.

Ideal conditions Outgoing tide with southwesterly to southeasterly winds.

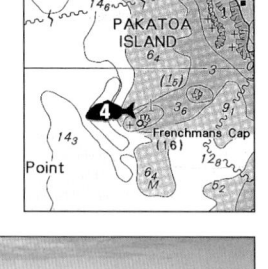

Rotoroa Island

Winter

In winter, the summer spots will still produce some good fishing in the right conditions and moon phases. However, it is more effective to target the resident snapper close in to the shoreline by straylining. These are seldom large but fish up to 3 kg are quite common. As usual, targeting one spot and using berley and groundbait (see 'Berley and Groundbait', page 32) is a lot more productive than moving from spot to spot.

Pakatoa Reef

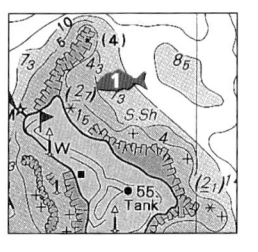

Fishing the incoming tide on the eastern side of the reef will ensure that the berley trail drops over and past the entire reef. Kingfish sometimes show up in the berley trail, and dusk fishing produces pan-size snapper with the occasional bigger fish.

Ideal conditions Incoming tide with northerly to northeasterly winds.

Pakatoa Foul

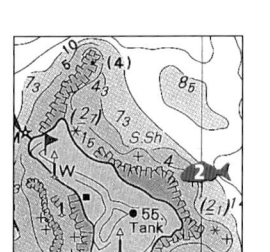

Foul ground (including a couple of submerged rocks) extends from the southeastern end of Pakatoa Island.

Ideal conditions Incoming tide with northerly to northeasterly winds (northern side), or outgoing tide with southwesterly to southeasterly winds (southern side).

Mussel Farm

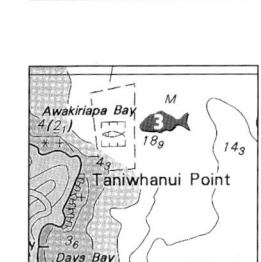

This is like a man-made reef and the huge amount of food here means it is a natural place to find snapper. The snapper are mostly small, pan-size fish and a lot of undersize fish also rip at the baits. Be sure to use 7/0 hooks so as not to gut-hook these small fish.

Ideal conditions Incoming tide with northwesterly to northeasterly winds (northern side), or outgoing tide with southwesterly to southeasterly winds (south side).

Rotoroa Island (1)

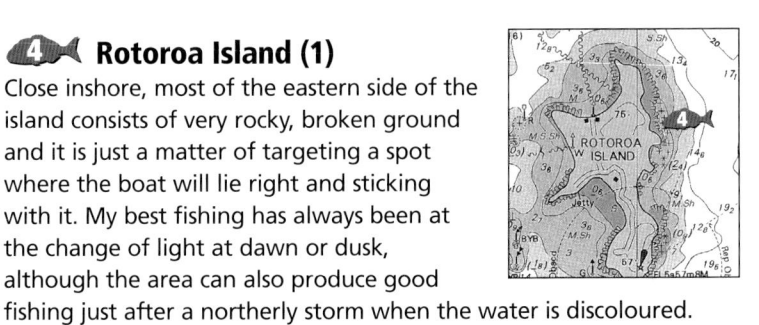

Close inshore, most of the eastern side of the island consists of very rocky, broken ground and it is just a matter of targeting a spot where the boat will lie right and sticking with it. My best fishing has always been at the change of light at dawn or dusk, although the area can also produce good fishing just after a northerly storm when the water is discoloured.

Ideal conditions Incoming tide with northerly to northeasterly winds, or outgoing tide with southerly to southeasterly winds.

Rotoroa Island (2)

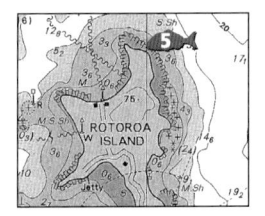

The northeast end of the island has a large kelp bed around the shoreline. Use lots of groundbait and berley.

Ideal conditions Incoming tide with northerly winds.

Rotoroa Reef

This is a triangular reef structure that can be fished from all sides, depending on the direction of the wind and tide. Mostly only pan-size fish hang around this structure, but I have been busted off by a very large snapper on more than one occasion.

Ideal conditions Incoming tide (north side) northwest to northeast winds, outgoing (south side) southwest to southeast winds.

Area  Waiheke Channel and Ponui Island

Habitat

The sea floor in the Waiheke Channel and the waters surrounding Ponui Island is mainly sand and mud, and the only major reef structures are Sunday Rock and those off Southwest Bay (Rotoroa) and in Ruthe Passage. The strong tidal flows bring in nutrient-rich water from the Tamaki Strait, giving life to the bottom-dwelling crabs, worms and shellfish and to the large numbers of baitfish that inhabit the area. The sea floor in the surrounding areas is largely flat, but there are a number of holes, up to 29 m deep. From Ruthe Passage around to Scullys Reef is plenty of foul ground with submerged rocks and reefs. At times, many of the shallow muddy bays also have good stocks of flounder.

North end of Ponui at its western end

Caution: not to be used for navigation.

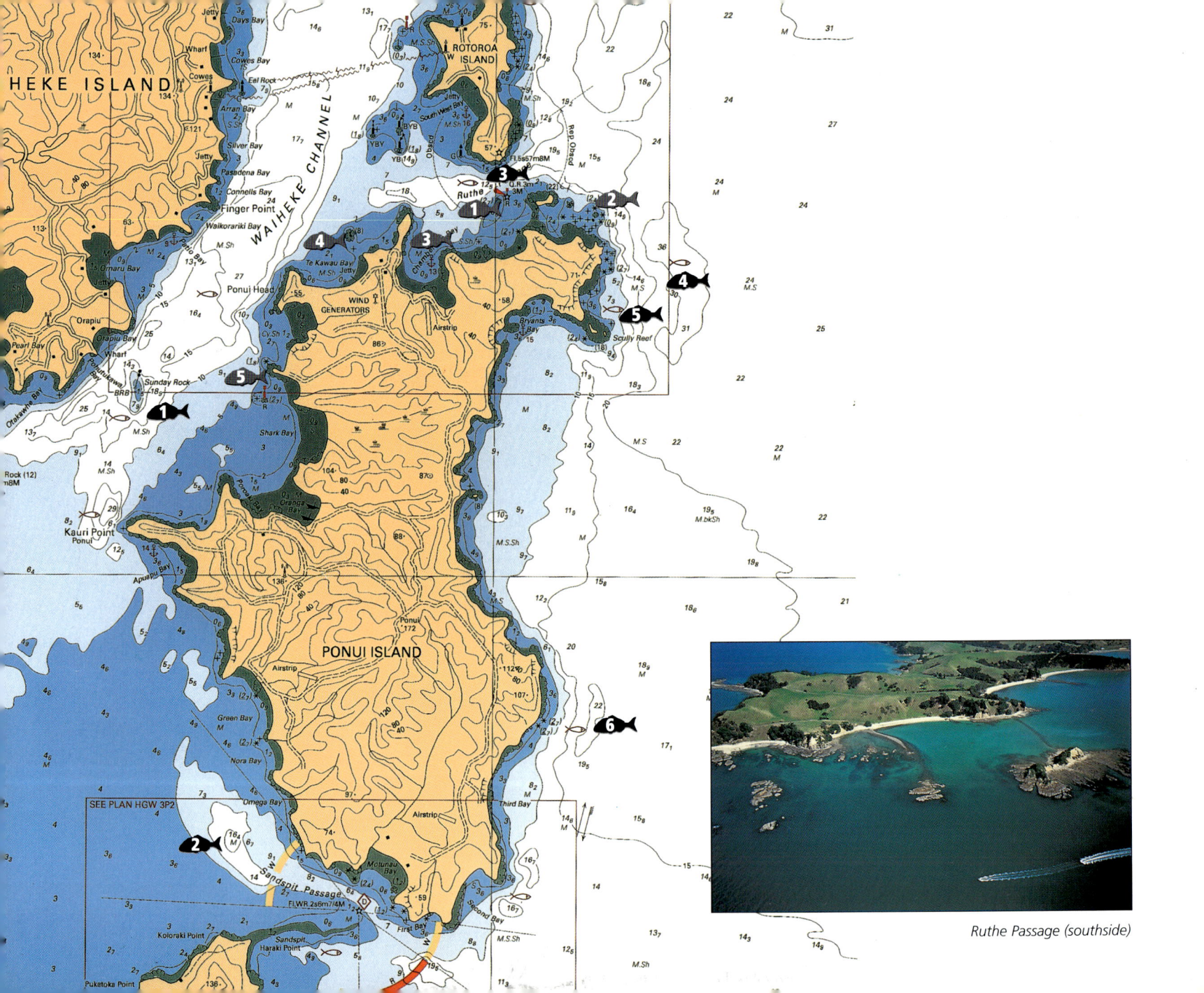

Ruthe Passage (southside)

Summer

Owing to the strong tidal flows, a lot of snapper migrate past here to the Tamaki Strait to feed. There are many deep holes and, at times, it can be difficult to decide where to fish. A quick drift fish using a baited flasher rig is often the best way to see what size snapper are about (the signs on the sounder can be misleading, as it is easy to mistake snapper for very dense schools of baitfish). To prevent baits being ripped to bits by the small snapper when bottom fishing back into these holes, use firmer ones such as squid, kahawai or mullet instead.

1 Sunday Rock

Spend a little time looking right around the rock prior to anchoring as the snapper aren't always in the same place. The fishing is often slow here, but although it may take a few hours it is fairly consistent.

Ideal conditions Incoming tide with northerly to northeasterly winds (northern side), or outgoing tide with southwesterly to south-southwesterly winds (southern side).

2 Sandspit Passage

South of Omega Bay is a 16.4-m hole surrounded by a very shallow area. A lot of snapper can often be seen feeding in the current on the bottom or along the sides of this hole when the tide is in full flood. Use a running sinker rig with long traces.

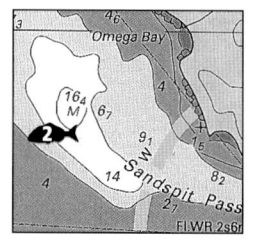

Ideal conditions Incoming tide with easterly to southeasterly winds, or outgoing tide with northwesterly to westerly winds.

3 Ruthe Passage

This is a fairly narrow passage of water that can get quite boisterous in summer as a result of the large number of passing boats. At times, the fishing can be fast and furious, but it is usually fairly slow, especially when there is little tide running. An outgoing tide is generally the best time to fish, and the best rig to use is a running sinker with a 1–2-m trace.

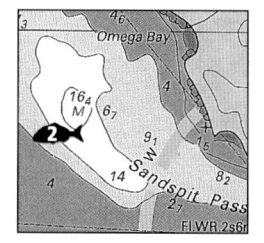

Ideal conditions Incoming tide with easterly winds, or outgoing tide with westerly to southwesterly winds.

4 Ponui Hole

East of the northern tip of Ponui is a deep hole ranging from 31 m to 36 m. This is a good place to set a longline as the bottom consists of sand. On an incoming tide the fish are often found on the drop-off at the northern end of the hole or right on the rise at the southern end.

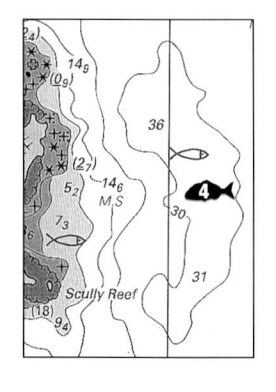

Ideal conditions Incoming tide with northerly to northeasterly winds, or outgoing tide with southerly to southeasterly winds.

5 Scully Reef

A good berley trail can make for some dynamite fishing. Big snapper are best targeted with big fresh baits at dusk.

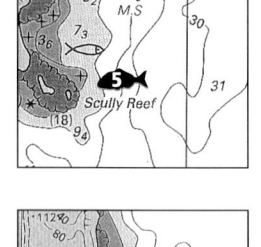

Ideal conditions Incoming tide with north to northeast winds, outgoing tide south to southwest winds.

6 22-Metre Finger

The depression will hold fish most of the time but the area really fires up in the late afternoon.

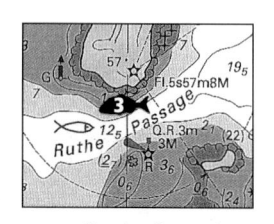

Ideal conditions Incoming tide northerly winds, outgoing tide with southerly winds.

Winter

Targeting winter snapper in this area can be quite hard and as a consequence you need to put in the time and effort. The most effective method is straylining close to the rocky shore with lots of berley and groundbait. When fishing this area in winter, ensure the stern of the boat is facing the target area as it is critical to set a pattern of baits in the berley trail (see 'Straylining', page 26).

➊ Ruthe Passage

The reef on the southern side of the passage is an ideal habitat for winter snapper. Anchor at the western end so that the stern of the boat is facing the rocks, not the open channel. Keep a constant berley trail going and cast baits out towards the inside and end of the reef.

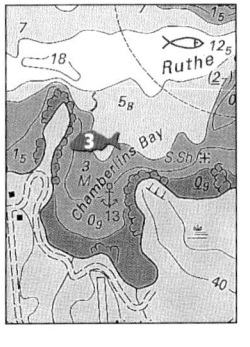

Ideal conditions Outgoing tide with northwesterly to westerly winds.

➋ The Broken Foul

There is a huge area of broken foul and exposed reef structure on the starboard side as you exit Ruthe Passage to the east, and extreme care must be taken when anchoring here. Target the resident snapper by

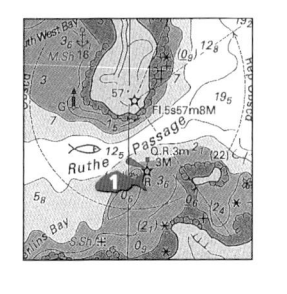

straylining unweighted baits cast in a pattern well astern (see 'Straylining', page 26) as the incoming tide will take your berley and groundbait well up into the rocks and kelp.

Ideal conditions Incoming tide with northerly to northeasterly winds.

The Broken Foul

➌ Chamberlins Bay

When the wind is blowing hard from the south, the southern side of the bay is sheltered by the headland. The shoreline is covered in seaweed and it is often possible to pick up a few pan-size snapper as they feed in the area. Chamberlins Bay is also renowned for piper; to catch them, anchor anywhere in the bay and cast out small baited hooks (see 'All About Bait', page 18).

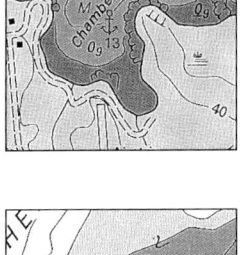

➍ Te Kawau Bay Rock

At the northern end of Te Kawau Bay is a large exposed rock, which can be fished from either side depending on the tide. Anchor so that the stern of the boat is facing the middle of the rock (not the end) or the tide will take the baits away. My best snapper

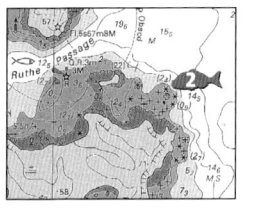

here have all been taken on fresh piper, straylined at dusk and dawn.

Ideal conditions Incoming tide with north-northeasterly winds (eastern side), or outgoing tide with southerly to southwesterly winds (western side).

➎ Shark Bay

The rock at the north end of the bay is a good backstop when the fishing is hard. Very seldom do we not catch fish here, but they are generally only small pannies. Berley and groundbait is a must here.

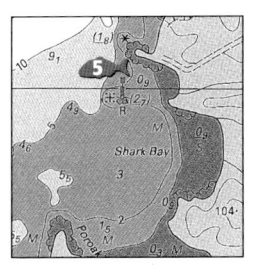

Ideal conditions Incoming tide with northerly winds, outgoing tide with southerly winds.

Area ⑮ Firth of Thames

Habitat

This vast area of water is a very significant part of the Hauraki Gulf for breeding snapper. The upper reaches of the Firth are very shallow and harbour huge areas of mangroves that offer food and protection for juvenile fish. Feeding into these mangroves are three rivers — the Waitakaruru, Piako and Waihou — which enrich the area with mud and silt and provide an ideal habitat for large numbers of crabs and worms. The bottom of the Firth is very flat and shelves slowly into deeper water off the Waimangu Point area. Mud, sand and broken shell make up the bottom and the area is rich in crabs, oysters and both mussels and horse mussels. As a result, this is the perfect habitat for flounder, which are fished commercially, and also for stingrays and sharks. Because this is such an important breeding ground, longliners are banned until the end of the spawning season. Inexperienced boaties should be aware that the Firth can be a very dangerous stretch of water, particularly in strong winds with opposing tides. It is an area that should always be treated with respect when fishing.

Pakatoa Island

Caution: not to be used for navigation.

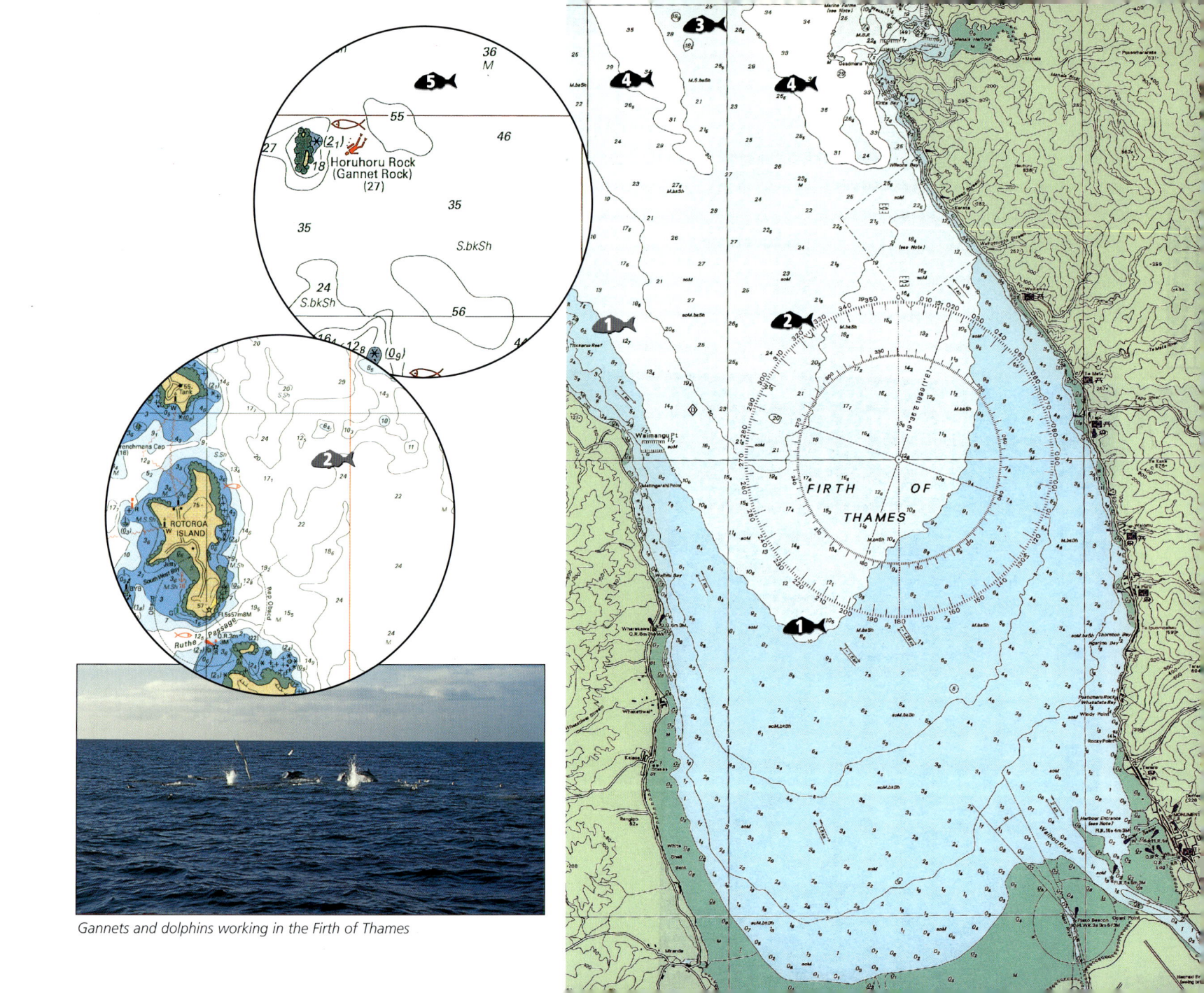

Gannets and dolphins working in the Firth of Thames

Summer

The schools of breeding snapper arrive in the outer Firth and then slowly work their way into its upper reaches. Once they have spawned, the snapper keep feeding and move right up into the shallows. Commercial flounder fishermen often see big snapper feeding in the mangroves in water so shallow that the fishes' backs are exposed. The snapper are often in schools whose members are all of a uniform size, with only the odd fish being much larger or smaller than the others. Therefore, if you are plagued by undersized snapper, it is best to move rather than stay and end up harming a lot of small fish. Use more groundbait than berley in this area as berley will attract sharks, whereas small pieces of bait will not have quite the same effect. At the start of the spawning season (from October onwards), smaller cut baits can be a lot more effective than big baits such as whole pilchards. This is because snapper pick at their natural food and there is little tidal run to work them up into a competitive feeding frenzy. Straylining works best in the upper reaches, where the shallow water and lack of strong tides often mean that sinkers are not required at all.

1 The Upper Reaches

The upper reaches have no reef structures to hold snapper but, in the areas with mussels along the western shore, some bigger fish can be found. Where the contour line comes to a point and the depth changes from 10 m to 8 m, there is a tidal run of 1–1.5 knots. As always, fishing when the tide and wind are running in the same direction is best.

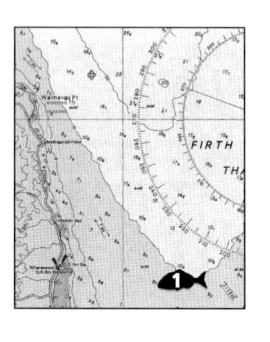

Ideal conditions Incoming tide with westerly to northerly winds (fish back up the bank), or outgoing tide with easterly to southwesterly winds.

2 The Rise

From Waimangu Point across the Firth to Waikawau on the Coromandel side, the bottom drops to 20–25 m with a small rise of 19.3 m in the middle. Snapper often hold on and around this rise and can really come on the bite on the incoming tide at dusk. Longlining can be effective here, although the area is full of stingrays and sharks.

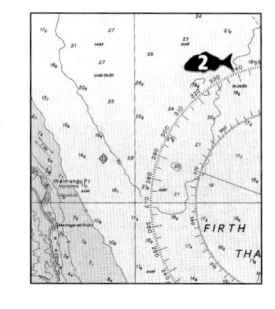

Ideal conditions Incoming tide with northwesterly to northerly winds, or outgoing tide with southwesterly to southerly winds.

3 The Pinnacles

Take a line from the north end of Ponui Island to Deadmans Point on the Coromandel Peninsula and look for two pinnacles of reef rising to 19.9 m and 18.5 m. These are fairly large areas of reef and often hold a lot of fish. Have a good look at the whole reef structure prior to dropping anchor (see 'Deep-water Fishing', page 34). It is important to use berley (in a weighted bag just off the bottom) and groundbait — at times when I have been full on there have been boats a mere 50 m away from mine that were not catching fish simply because they were not berleying.

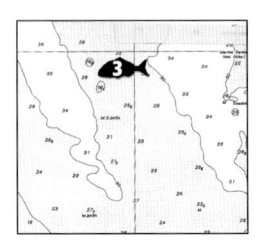

Ideal conditions Incoming tide with northwesterly to northerly winds, or outgoing tide with southwesterly to southerly winds.

4 The Banks

Cross the Firth with the sounder set on zoom, watching closely when the bottom starts to drop away. Snapper are often found on the edges of the banks, and baited flasher and ledger rigs are an effective way to target them. This is a good way to build up an understanding of snapper movements in deeper water while increasing your local knowledge.

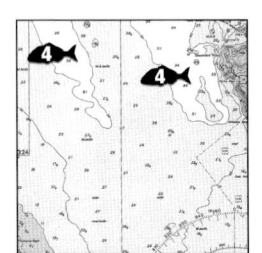

🐟 North of Gannet Rock

From as early as October, larger schools of snapper in the 4–6-kg range are often found 4–8 miles north to northeast of Gannet Rock. As the bottom is flat here, slowly work the area with the sounder until you find the fish and then either anchor or drift fish through them.

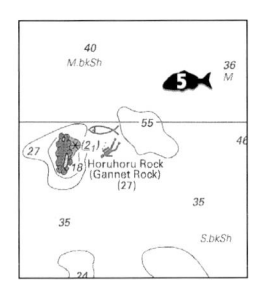

Winter

Depending on the water temperature and the amount of feed on the bottom, large amounts of snapper often spend the whole winter in the Firth and so a lot of the summer spots also work well at this time. Not many snapper are found in the shallows — they tend to be very spread out, so a good sounder will prove invaluable in finding them. Setting a longline is always a good way of covering your bases in the outer Firth during winter (see 'Longlining', page 42). The bottom is largely free of any snags and it is often possible to set a longline when it is too uncomfortable to anchor. This method can be very effective here and you may be surprised by the size of some of the snapper you catch. While waiting for the longline to work (generally about an hour or so), try straylining in the calmer waters close to shore.

🐟 Orere Point

Titokarua Reef is a large area of submerged rocks and foul. Anchor so that the stern of the boat is to the foul and use berley and groundbait. Strayline half-baits back into the foul. Just out from the western side of the reef is a 5.7-m hole. Anchor so that your baits fall into this area.

Ideal conditions Incoming tide with easterly to northeasterly winds, or outgoing tide with westerly to southwesterly winds.

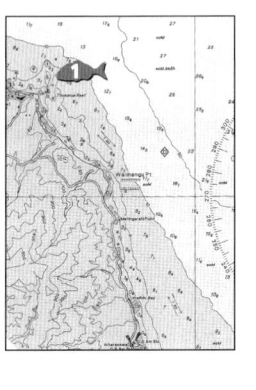

🐟 The Rises

About a mile or two east of the gap between Pakatoa and Rotoroa islands, the bottom rises to 12.5 m, 6.4 m, 10.3 m, 10 m and 11 m. Use the sounder to have a good look around these rises and in the areas between them. The snapper that winter over in this area can be quite nice 2–4-kg fish. Fish back up to these rises with the tide using a weighted berley bag just off the bottom and keep up a constant flow of groundbait. Things can be slow to start at times but, when the berley and groundbait take effect, the fishing can really speed up.

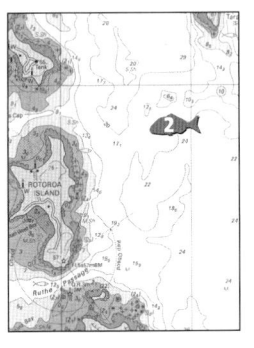

Ideal conditions Incoming tide with north-northwesterly to north-northeasterly winds, or outgoing tide with southerly to southeasterly winds.

Habitat

This area is made up of many islands, rocks and reefs, all of which provide an ideal habitat for snapper. The bottom is largely muddy sand and broken shell, and is home to crabs, worms and shellfish. The waters are very rich in nutrients, which is one of the reasons why there are so many mussel farms in the area. These farms provide a bonus for fisherman targeting snapper as they add huge amounts of available food to the area. When the mussels are being harvested, the water discolours as the lines are stripped, and dislodged crabs and small mussels create a giant berley trail. The upper reaches of the harbours are very shallow and support lots of mangroves, which provide both food and protection for very young snapper. Baitfish such as koheru, piper and sprats are easily caught here, and an added bonus is that mullet can be netted along much of the shoreline.

Coromandel Islands

Caution: not to be used for navigation.

Elephant Cove

Mussel farm

Summer

The influx of spawning snapper starts in October and the schools often come close in to shore. It pays to take the time to study a chart of this area thoroughly as the contour of the bottom changes quite dramatically and includes some very deep holes. This is where a chart plotter can be a very useful tool, making it easy follow the contours and to see where the snapper are schooling. When the tides are very strong snapper hold in the deep holes and channels, and schools of spawning snapper can often be found to the west of the islands where the bottom starts rising from 38 m. Drift fishing using baited flasher and ledger rigs is a good way to learn about the area. It is a hugely fishable stretch, and by using a plotter and sounder it is possible to check out different water depths without travelling very far.

❶ Black Rocks

Note the five deep holes close to the rocks. Use running rigs with 1–2-m traces or ledger rigs, and anchor so that you can fish back down into the holes with a weighted berley bag just off the bottom.

Ideal conditions Incoming tide with northwesterly to northeasterly winds, or outgoing tide with southwesterly to southeasterly winds.

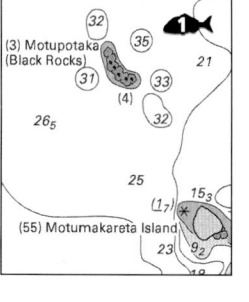

❷ The Hole

Between Double Island and Bush Island the bottom drops from 17.6 m to 27.5 m and then comes back up to 17.6 m. Ledger or running rigs are best here.

Ideal conditions Incoming tide with northwesterly to northeasterly winds, or outgoing tide with southerly to southeasterly winds.

❸ Cow and Calf

Schools of snapper are often found right around these two islands, although some of my best fishing has been in 12 m of water between them.

Ideal conditions Incoming tide with northeasterly to northwesterly winds and outgoing tides with southwesterly to southeasterly winds.

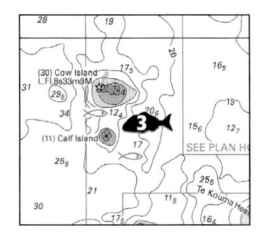

The Cow and Calf

Winter

Each year is slightly different but, with the huge amount of food in the area, the snapper are also often found in the summer spots. There are fewer fish around in winter but they can be of a better size: up to 4–6 kg at times. Straylining is the best way to target the local snapper at this time as the many islands and reefs offer fishing opportunities in any wind direction. These shorelines and rocky areas also feature lots of dense kelp and good tidal flows, and this helps to hold the snapper. As usual, the use of berley and groundbait will help to bring the snapper on the bite during the colder months.

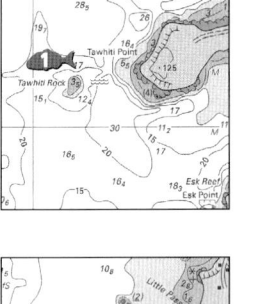

🐟 Tawhiti Rock

This rock comes up to 3.5 m and, between it and Tawhiti Point, the tidal flows are strong, often causing overfalls. Generally speaking, the snapper are found around the rock, although at times the fishing in the strong rip can be great.

Ideal conditions Incoming tide with northwesterly to northeasterly winds, or outgoing tide with southerly to southeasterly winds.

🐟 Deep Cove

I have sheltered here out of strong winds and straylined on to the western shoreline with very good results. Tide direction makes no difference, but fresh piper baits (which can be caught in Deep Cove) catch the bigger fish. Often the best results are to be had at dawn or dusk.

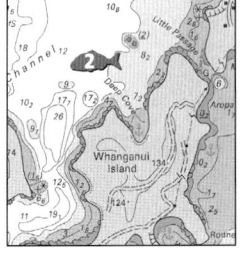

🐟 Deep Cove Reef

Due north of Deep Cove is a reef that is exposed at low tide. This fishes just as well on either the incoming or outgoing tide — you only have to anchor so that the stern of the boat is facing the middle of the reef. Cast baits towards and upcurrent of the rock so that the tide drags them down past the kelp.

Ideal conditions Incoming tide with northeasterly to northerly winds (north side), or outgoing tide with southwesterly to southerly winds (south side).

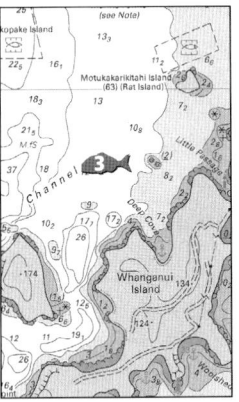

🐟 Hautapu Rocks

This area can either fish very well, with lots of good-sized snapper, or it can deliver a plague of small fish. If all you are getting is undersize snapper, try another part of the reef instead. The 32-m hole just out from the marker is also worth a look.

Ideal conditions Incoming tide with northwesterly to northerly winds, or outgoing tide with southerly to southwesterly winds.

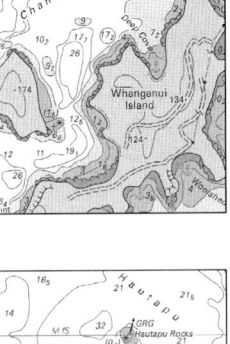

Area 17 Top of the Coromandel Peninsula

Habitat

The huge amount of water that passes through this area with each tide brings out nutrients from the inner Hauraki Gulf and Firth of Thames, so baitfish, kahawai and kingfish are plentiful. The shoreline and submerged reefs are covered with kelp and are home to kina, crabs, snails and crayfish (big snapper love crayfish!). There are a couple of magnificent sandy beaches and, when no swell is running, these are a great place to drag a bait net for piper. Some of the biggest piper I have seen were caught in Port Jackson. It is hard to break this area into summer and winter spots, both because the fishing is so good all year round and because trips are limited owing to distance and weather constraints. The secret to success lies in choosing a spot and sticking to it; anglers who struggle to catch fish up here are the ones who move about all the time. I once anchored on one reef all day, groundbaited heavily and consistently caught snapper; by the end of the tide run I was releasing big snapper, all over 5 kg. The berley trail and constant groundbaiting brought and held snapper close to the boat — if I had shifted about, I would not have had the same results (see 'Deep-water Fishing', page 34). Just before I left, a boat anchored 100 m away from me and yet caught only 1–2-kg snapper, proving again that time and effort with berley pay big dividends.

Channel Island

Play it Safe

The top of the Coromandel Peninsula is a very long way from any launching ramp and you have to cross a lot of open water to reach it. Such a trip is not for inexperienced boaties, and ideally you should always go in the company of other boats, taking additional fuel and food in case the weather turns foul and you have to take shelter — in such conditions it is better to stay put than risk lives. Tidal flows around the top end of the peninsula can be very strong, creating overfalls on the surface even in calm conditions. I have seen the wind pick up on the turn of the tide and, in less than 20 minutes, build seas to a state where they were breaking over the bow of a 10-m launch. Although the area's remoteness limits the number of days when it can safely be reached, the fishing is stunning so it pays to watch for a weather window when planning a trip.

Caution: not to be used for navigation.

cS.bkSh

44

62

S.bkSh ← ⊢⊢⊢⊢ 1 to 2 kn

33

60

44

9

46

29

8

42

Channel Island
Fl (2) 12s 79m 9M

10

bkSh

58

36

55

55

36

55

36

47

2 to 3 kn

31

5

19₅

38

30

19₅

42

46

55

49

4

35

7

Cape Colville

27

(27)

25

6

Square Top Island (75)

.bkSh

31

Port

14₆

2

4 9 13₁

8₅

6 7

22

14₃ 10₃

2₁

3 31

7

2₁

7

40

The Pinnacles (100)

Jackson

24

4 6

0 9

219

Sugar Loaf Rocks 44

18₃

1

12₅

⚓

29

+

Caiiti Point

0 9

4

0 9

256·

50

2₁

33

31

5 8

0 6

188.

Port Jackson

100

7 6

Poley Bay

40

24

195·

Muriwai Stream

200

22

Pahi Stream

300

43

+

400

35
Point

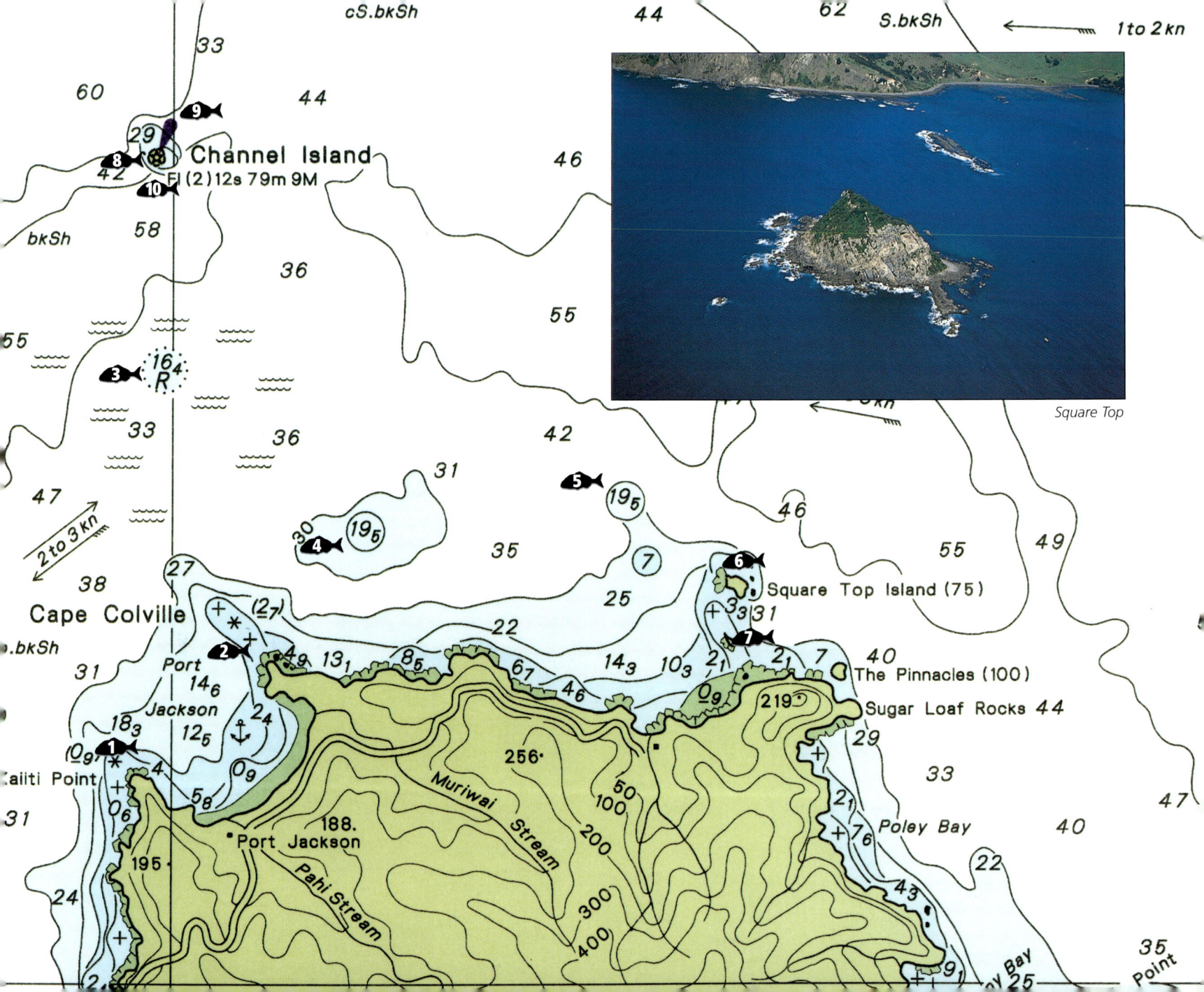

Square Top

①➤ Port Jackson Reef

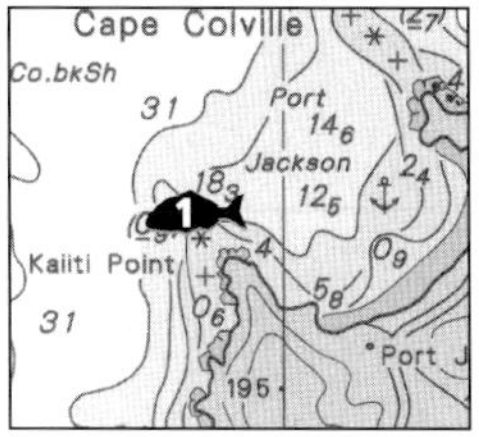

The western headland of Port Jackson has many rocks and reef structures, including a large rock that is exposed at low tide. Fish back between the rock and the headland.

Ideal conditions Incoming tide with northeasterly to easterly winds (east side of headland), or outgoing tide with southwesterly to southerly winds (west side of headland).

②➤ Jackson Reef

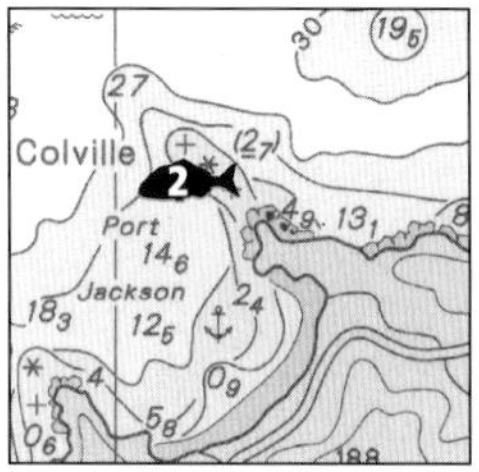

This extends well out from the eastern headland and has a strong tidal flow running past it. It is best fished close to the headland, preferably at dusk.

Ideal conditions Incoming tide with northerly to northeasterly winds (east side), or outgoing tide with westerly to northwesterly winds (west side).

③➤ Cape Colville Pinnacle

Northwest of Cape Colville (approximately 1.5 miles offshore) is a large structure that rises from 33 m to 16.4 m. The tidal flow is very fast here and so this is not a place to fish on spring tides. Anchor back off the rock so that you fish back up the face of it. A ledger rig or a sinker on a trace rig is best. Use a berley bag off the anchor rope.

Ideal conditions Incoming tide with northeasterly to easterly winds (east side of rock), or outgoing tide with westerly to southwesterly winds (west side of rock).

④➤ Cape Colville Reef

Between Cape Colville and Square Top Island is a large area of reef that rises to 19.5 m. Have a good look around before anchoring (see 'Deep-water Fishing', page 34) and add a berley bag to the anchor line. Groundbait right

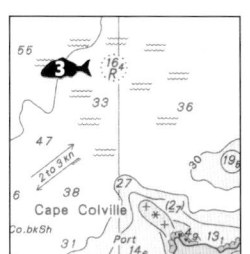

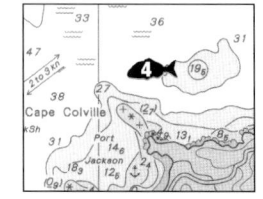

Jackson Reef

over the tide and stick to the one spot. I have caught some big snapper here using monster baits (see 'Successful Straylining Rigs', page 22).

Ideal conditions Incoming tide with northeasterly to easterly winds, or outgoing tide with northwesterly to westerly winds.

5 Square Top Island Reef (1)

Northwest of Square Top Island is an area of reef structure, one pinnacle of which comes up to 7 m and another, just under a mile further out, to 19.5 m. Take time to check out the whole area before anchoring, and stick to the one spot.

Ideal conditions Incoming tide with easterly to northeasterly winds, or outgoing tide with westerly to southwesterly winds.

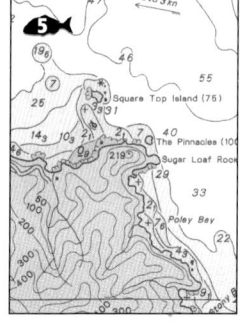

6 Square Top Island

There is a finger of exposed rock jutting out from the northwestern end of Square Top Island. Strayline back into the rocks, from the head into the bay.

Ideal conditions Incoming tide with northerly to northeasterly winds.

7 Square Top Island Reef (2)

The shoreline directly in from Square Top Island features a large reef structure, some of it exposed. Either side of this is perfect for straylining.

Ideal conditions Incoming tide with northerly to northeasterly winds (east side of reef), or outgoing tide with westerly to southwesterly winds (west side).

8 Channel Island (1)

Between Channel Island and the rock is a great straylining spot. Cast big baits back into the gap so that they float down through the white water.

Ideal conditions Outgoing tide with westerly to southwesterly winds.

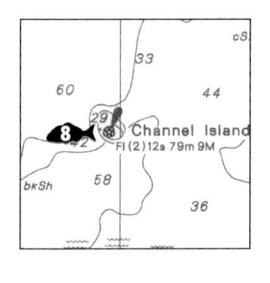
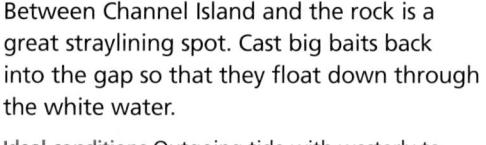

9 Channel Island (2)

There is a rock that comes up to approximately 7 m on the northwestern side of the island. Anchor in the gap between the rock and the island approximately 100 m out.

Ideal conditions Outgoing tide with westerly winds.

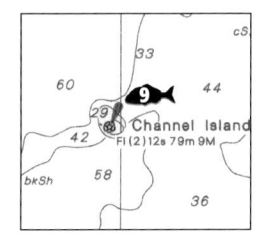

10 Channel Island (3), or Phil's Big Fish Spot

Anchor about 35 m offshore in 27 m of water midway along the eastern side of the island. The bottom should drop off to 45 m just behind the boat. Use big baits and drop them slowly back in the current.

Ideal conditions Incoming tide with northerly to northeasterly winds.

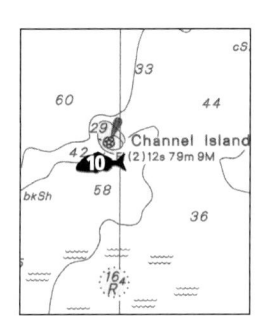

Area ⑱ Little Barrier

Habitat

Little Barrier Island lies approximately halfway between Kawau and Great Barrier islands and is exposed to winds and swells from all directions. Those with small boats should look carefully at the weather before embarking on a trip to Little Barrier and be sure to carry spare fuel; it is 14 miles to the nearest shelter if the weather turns nasty. Although it is okay to fish all around the island, Little Barrier is a wildlife sanctuary and so landing — even on the rocky outcrops — is forbidden. Owing to its isolation and exposure to the elements, there is not much fishing pressure here and therefore very little difference between summer and winter tactics. It is possible either to strayline in close or to deep-water fish the trenches all year round, weather permitting.

Ngatamahine Point

Caution: not to be used for navigation.

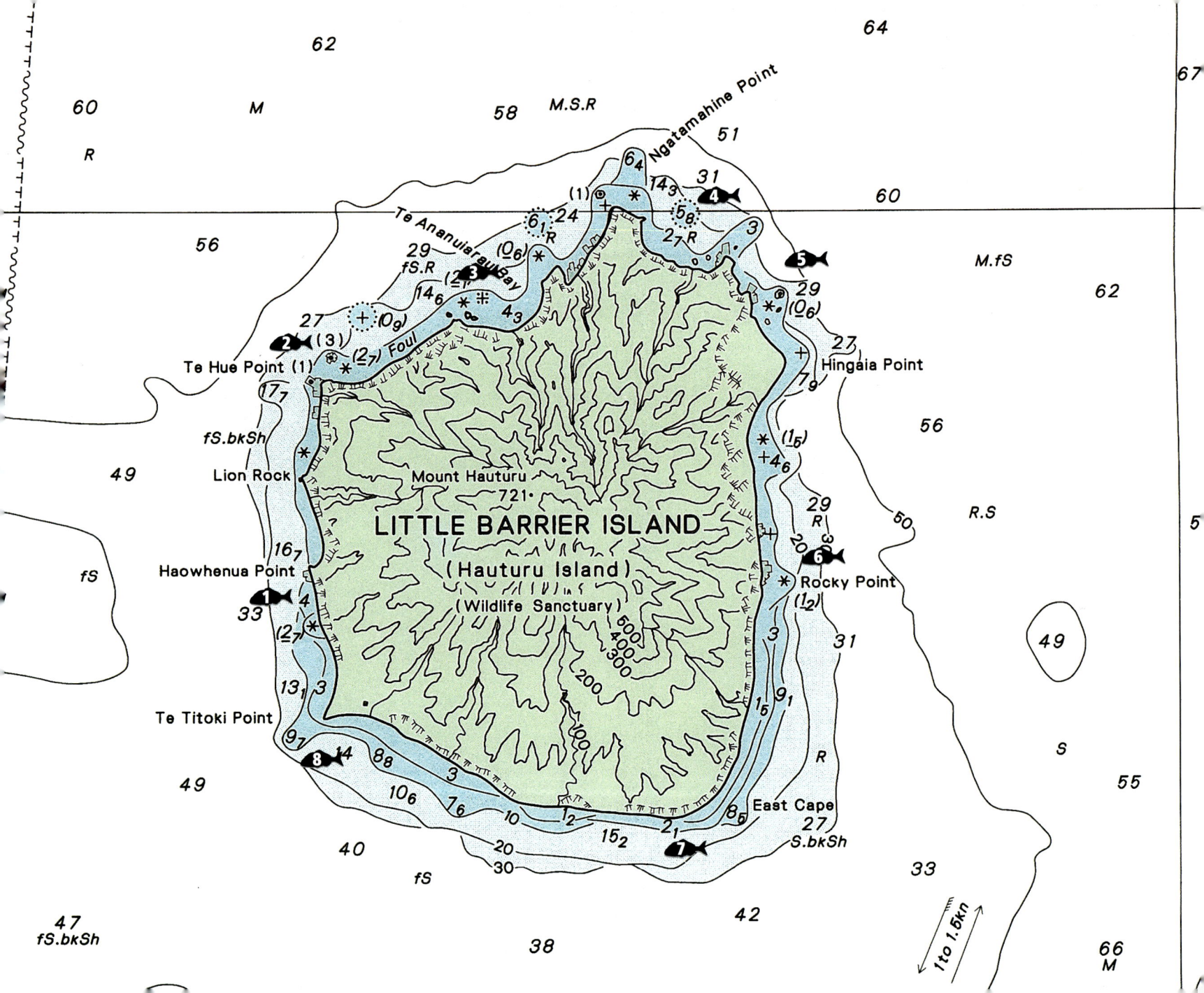

Deep-water Fishing

To the west of Little Barrier are a number of trenches, the drop-offs to which are visible on the chart as contour lines. They are easy to find using a sounder and plotter, and are worth exploring as there is a lot to be learnt here about the movements and habits of snapper schools. It is usually best to use baited flasher or ledger rigs or jigs, and extreme care is needed when anchoring as this area is directly in the path of the telecommunications cables.

Straylining

The sea floor only begins to rise about half a mile from the shore; beyond that it is relatively deep and the bottom consists of mud, sand and broken shell with the occasional small area of rock. The shoreline is very rocky, with big boulders in some places, and is heavily forested with dark brown kelp (this is why many of the snapper here have dark skin — for camouflage). Vast amounts of nutrient-rich water pass the island and it is fairly common to see big schools of kahawai and trevally feeding in the current lines and back eddies. There is also plenty of food here for snapper, especially in the kelp: limpets, crabs, snails and crayfish.

1 Te Titoki Point to Te Hue Point

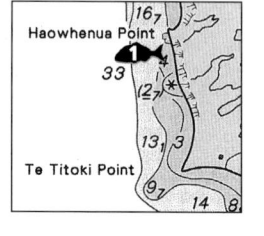

This shoreline is very kelpy, with just a couple of rocks that are awash. The cliffs give good protection from easterly winds and straylining is best at the change of light in the evening. A good, reliable spot for pan-size snapper.

Ideal conditions Incoming tide with northwesterly to westerly winds, or outgoing tide with southwesterly to southerly winds.

2 Te Hue Point

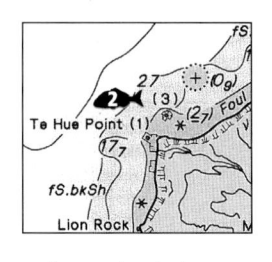

The broken rocks and submerged gutters provide a great habitat for both snapper and kingfish. The fishing is generally best on an incoming tide with a moderate swell breaking on the rocks. Use plenty of berley and groundbait.

Ideal conditions Incoming tide with northwesterly to northeasterly winds (northern side), or outgoing tide with southwesterly to southerly winds (southern side).

3 Te Hue Point to Ngatamahine Point

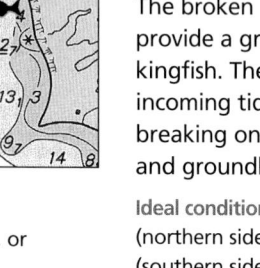

There are numerous submerged rocks and reefs along this rocky, kelpy shoreline, so great care must be taken when positioning the boat. Choose one spot and fish it over the whole tide.

Ideal conditions Incoming tide with northerly to northeasterly winds, or outgoing tide with southwesterly to westerly winds.

Te Titoki Point

⬤⬤ Ngatamahine Point to Waimaomao Bay

This area is often overlooked as there are so many other good spots around the island. However, some of the biggest snapper are caught here. It is worth targeting the rock that rises to 5.8 m in the middle of the bay, especially at dusk. Although much of the shoreline in the bay does not look 'fishy', some big snapper have been caught here in just a couple of metres of water. Be prepared to put in a fair amount of time, berley and groundbait to be successful.

Ideal conditions Incoming tide with northerly to northwesterly winds, or outgoing tide with southerly to southwesterly winds.

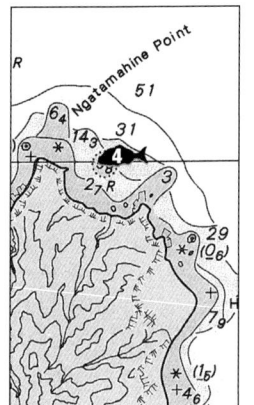

⬤⬤ Waimaomao Bay to Hingaia Point

This area features rocks that are both exposed and awash, and it is best to anchor so the baits can be cast to the edge of the white water. Again, choose one spot and stick to it over the whole tide. 'Walk' an unweighted bait back from the edge of the rocks into deeper water, and try a large monster bait (see 'All About Bait', page 18) on a lazy line to improve your chances of a really big snapper.

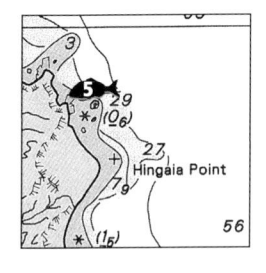

Ideal conditions Incoming tide with northerly to northwesterly winds, or outgoing tide with southerly to southwesterly winds.

⬤⬤ Hingaia Point to East Cape

Close to shore, the bottom is fairly bouldery with lots of kelp. Although better at producing crayfish than snapper, this area has yielded good fish when I have berleyed heavily and fished in the late afternoon and on into the dark.

Ideal conditions Incoming tide with northerly to northeasterly winds, or outgoing tide with southerly to southwesterly winds.

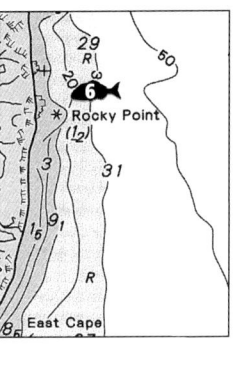
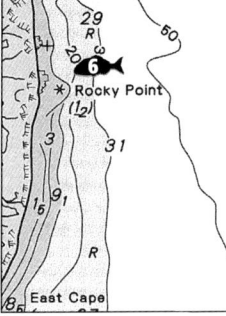

⬤⬤ East Cape to Te Titoki Point (East Cape End)

The whole shoreline here is one big kelp bed, with the best fishing found at either end. Use an unweighted bait to strayline back into the kelp, adding just enough weight to get the bait down as the tide increases.

Ideal conditions Outgoing tide with westerly to southwesterly winds.

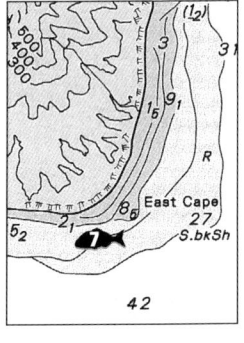
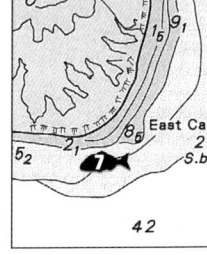

⬤⬤ East Cape to Te Titoki Point (Beach End)

A big kelp bed extends well out from the shoreline at the eastern end of the beach at Te Titoki Point. Strayline back to the edge of the kelp with a good berley trail at dusk.

Ideal conditions Outgoing tide with easterly to southeasterly winds.

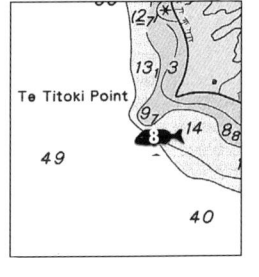

Area 19 Takatu Point to Flat Rock

Habitat

From the northern end of Takatu Point right down to Scow Point, the shoreline is very rugged with outcrops of rock (some of them quite isolated) and needs to be treated with some care. There are often strong tidal flows in the area and, if there is a swell from the northeasterly quarter, the sea here can get very rough, especially when the wind opposes the tide. Although the 'back', or eastern side, of Kawau Island is not quite so rugged, care is still needed close to the shore. However, out from the rocky shore, the bottom largely consists of sand and broken shell with the odd patch of low foul. There are also a number of isolated submerged rocks and these, combined with the more elaborate reef structure around Flat Rock, are an ideal habitat for big (sometimes very big) snapper. Kingfish and John Dory can also be found in good numbers in this area.

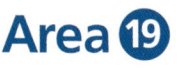

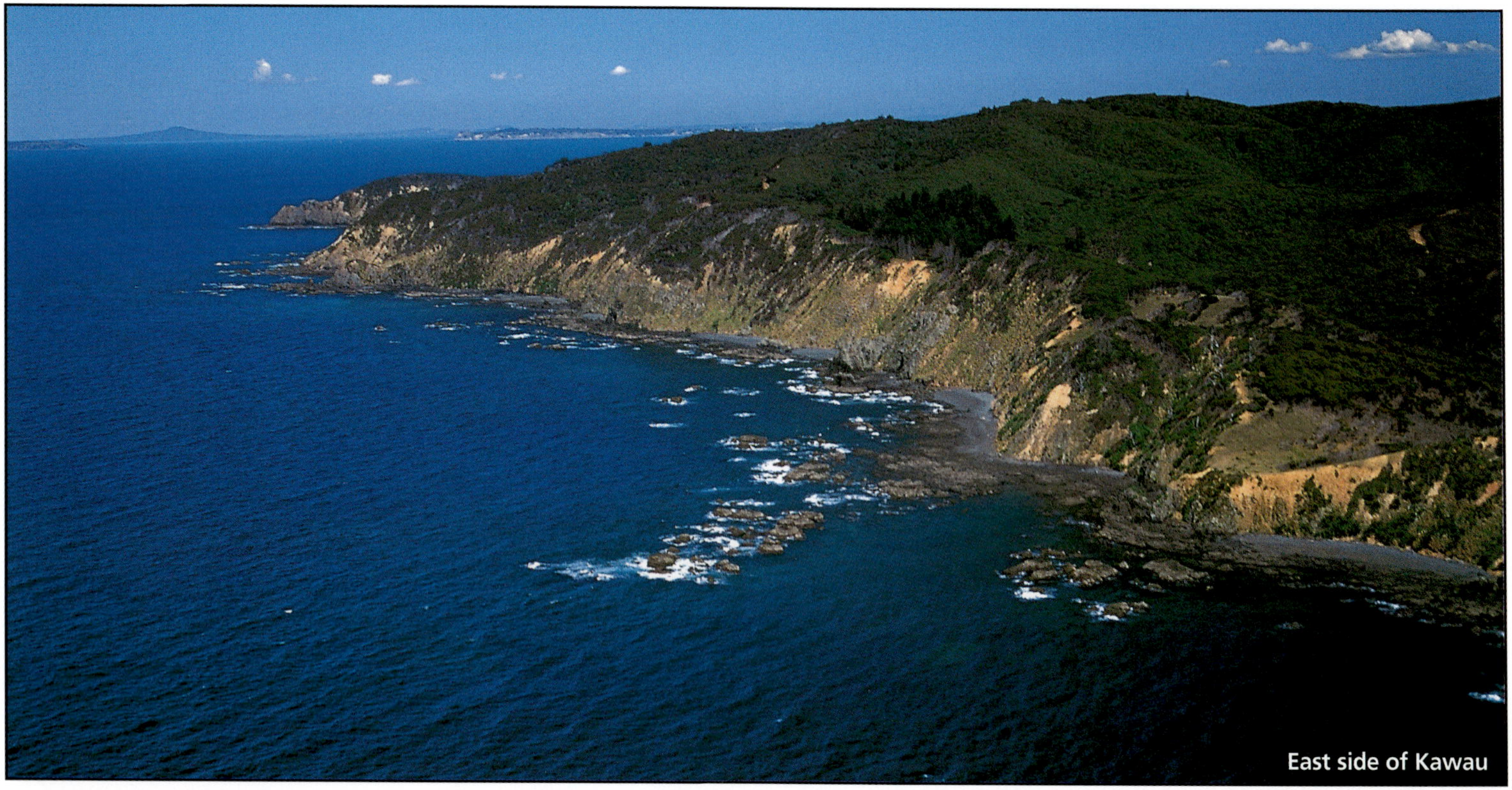
East side of Kawau

Caution: not to be used for navigation.

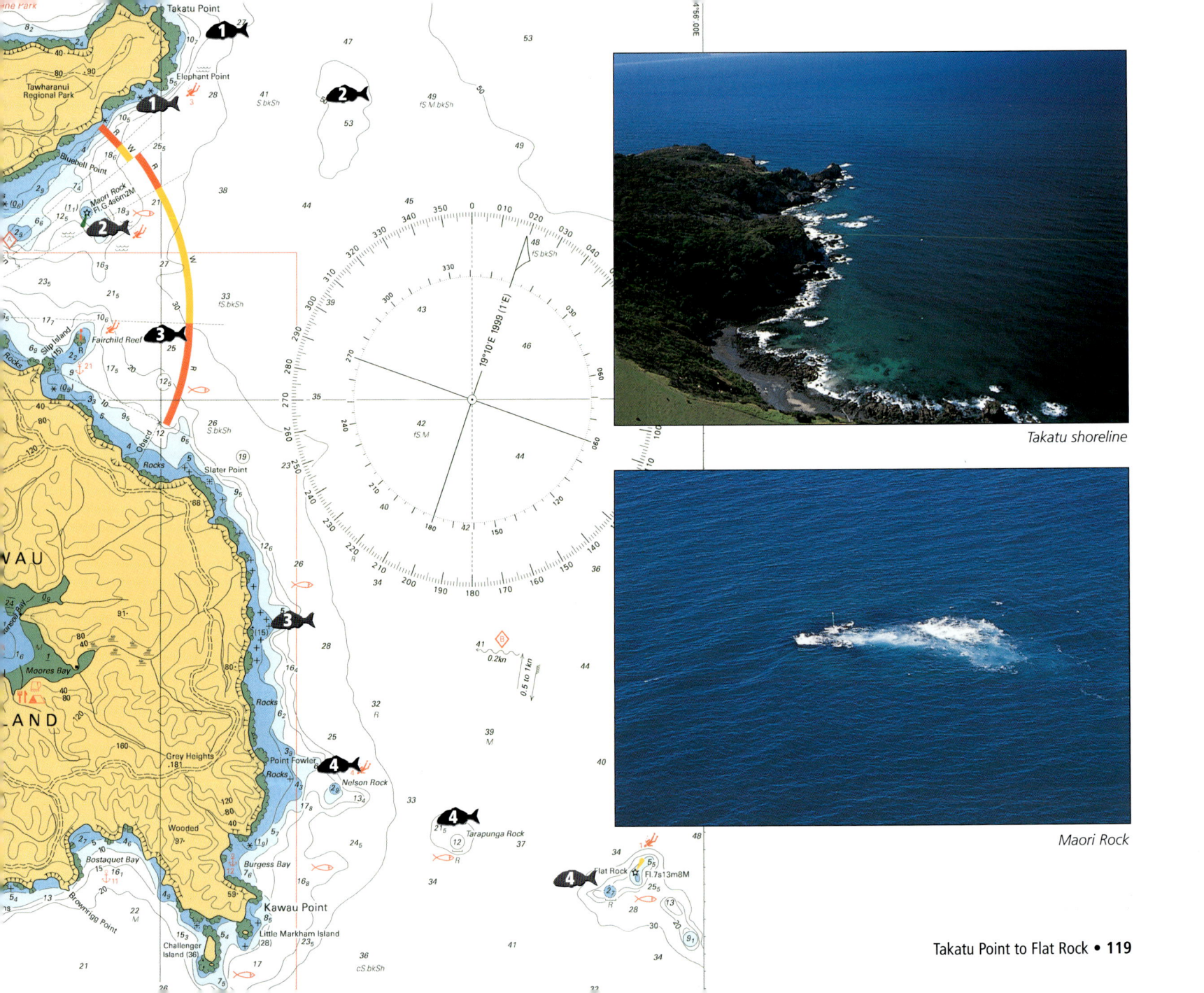

Takatu shoreline

Maori Rock

Summer

Pre-spawning snapper arrive in the area as early as September and can be found around the 30–40-m mark. It is also common to see flocks of gannets diving into baitfish work-ups in this area: drift through these with the sounder set on zoom and you will see snapper feeding on the scraps below. Jigging can be a very effective way to target these snapper as it mimics a wounded baitfish. Another option is to find some of the low foul around the 20–30-m mark, then anchor upcurrent (see 'Deep-water Fishing', page 34) and use a weighted berley bag set just off the bottom. Use groundbait to bring the snapper on the bite (especially at the change of light), and either a ledger or running rig with pilchards or strip baits of fresh kahawai.

1 Elephant Point

There is good fishing from the shore out to the 28-m mark in strong tidal flows. A weighted berley bag will help hold the fish in the area.

Ideal conditions Incoming tide with north-northwesterly to northeasterly winds, or outgoing tide with southwesterly to southeasterly winds.

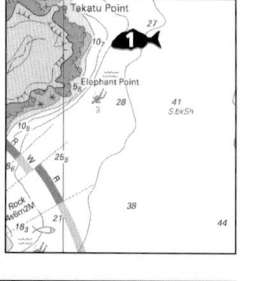

2 The 53-Metre Hole

This large hole lies due east of Elephant Point and is a good place to drift fish using ledger or flasher rigs.

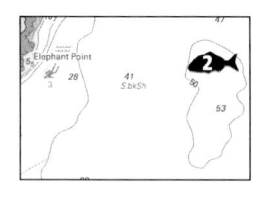

3 Low Foul

There are patches of low foul due east of Fairchild Reef in about 28 m that consistently fish well. Use lots of groundbait and try a monster bait (see 'Successful Straylining Rigs', page 22) to target a large snapper.

Ideal conditions Incoming tide with northwesterly to northeasterly winds, or outgoing tide with southwesterly to southeasterly winds.

4 Nelson Rock and Tarapunga Rock

These rocks will often produce big snapper and even the occasional monster. Do not anchor too close to the rocks as the trick is to fish back into the area where the snapper start to rise off the bottom.

Ideal conditions Incoming tide with northwesterly to northeasterly winds, or outgoing tide with southwesterly to southeasterly winds.

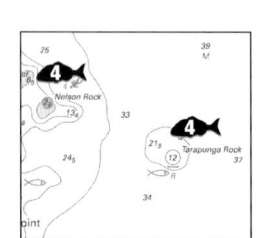

Elephant Point

Winter

I love fishing this area in winter as the summer spots often fish even better at this time of year. The vast areas of rocky shoreline hold lots of food and many snapper choose to winter over here. Choose one spot and stick to it, straylining close to shore with the tide so that your berley and groundbait (use lots of both) are spread into all of the nooks and crannies of this great snapper habitat.

① Elephant Point

South of the headland is a small bay with two submerged rocks. Ensure that conditions are calm and anchor back into the bay, between the rocks.

Ideal conditions Incoming tide with northeasterly to easterly winds, or outgoing tide with southerly to southeasterly winds.

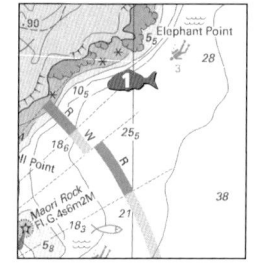

② Maori Rock

Care needs to be taken here as the strong tidal flows can cause dangerous overfalls. The southeastern side, where the reef is at 5.8 m, is best and berley and groundbait will make a huge difference.

Ideal conditions Incoming tide with northeasterly to easterly winds, or outgoing tide with westerly to southwesterly winds.

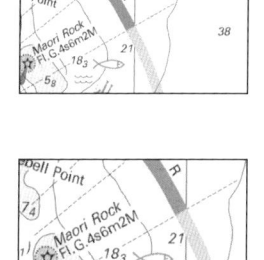

③ Slater Point to Point Fowler

This is my number one straylining spot, and I have caught and released lots of snapper up to 12 kg here. No one part of this shoreline seems any better than another, so the usual rules apply: select a spot, use lots of berley and groundbait, and stick with it. This is a great spot for a monster bait.

Ideal conditions Incoming tide with north-northwesterly to easterly winds, or outgoing tide with southerly to southwesterly winds.

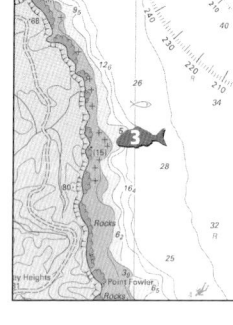

④ Flat Rock

At the north end, by the lighthouse, the bottom rises from 30 m and there are outcrops of rock to the west and southeast. Anchor close to but not on the reefs, or in the deep foul near the reef structure.

Ideal conditions Incoming tide with northwesterly to northeasterly winds (northern side), or outgoing tide with southwesterly to southeasterly winds (southern side).

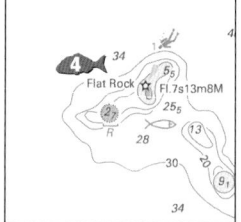

Flat Rock

The Mayne Islands

Habitat

Kawau Bay features a vast area of shallow water that extends from the mainland out to Kawau Island. Nearer the island, the tidal flow has created some deep channels and holes, the deepest of which drops to 24.5 m. The bottom largely consists of fine sand and broken shell, and is home to some of the snapper's favourite food: shellfish, crabs and worms. Although there is little kelp along the shorelines of either the mainland or Kawau, there is some seaweed growth on most of the rocky areas. The whole area holds lots of baitfish throughout the year, with piper in good numbers along the Kawau shoreline (try netting for them in the middle of the beach at Vivian Bay).

Caution: not to be used for navigation.

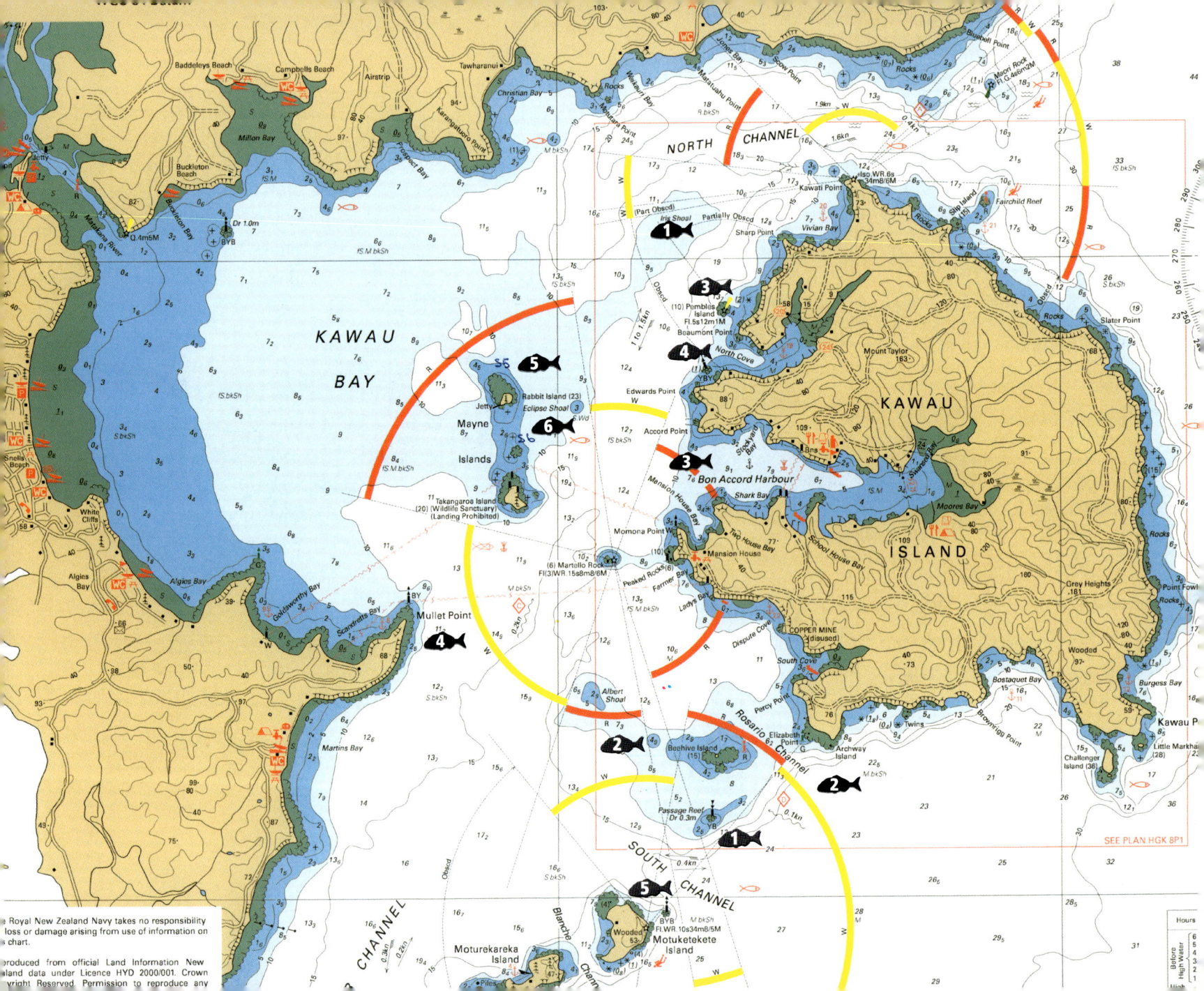

Summer

Although the pre-spawning snapper arrive on the outside of Kawau much earlier, they do not move into Kawau Bay in numbers until late November. Initially they stay in the channels, moving into the shallows in mid- to late December. Good schools can often be found close to shore, so a careful watch on the sounder can prove very worthwhile. At the height of the scallop season, lots of boats can be seen dredging in the Rosario Channel (between Beehive and Kawau) and on the Iris Shoal. The effect of this dredging is similar to the effect of a tractor ploughing a field: once the machinery has left and the noise has died down, out come the birds to feed on the exposed worms and grubs. It is similar here — once the boats have left, an evening fish over the recently dredged scallop beds can be very productive.

1 Iris Shoal Channel

This channel, between Sharp Point and Iris Shoal, drops to 19 m. Snapper come on the bite as the tide strengthens; use a running sinker or ledger rig.

Ideal conditions Incoming tide with northwesterly to northeasterly winds, or outgoing tide with southwesterly to southeasterly winds.

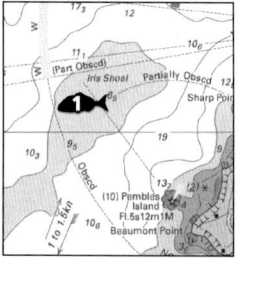

2 The 22-Metre Drop-off

Southwest of Rosario Channel, the bottom drops steeply to 22 m and snapper are often found on the edges or base of the drop-off.

Ideal conditions Outgoing tide with northwesterly winds.

3 Bon Accord Harbour

This is one of the most overlooked spots in the Gulf. Anchor right in the middle of the harbour entrance on the 10-m drop-off and be prepared to pull in lots of pan-size snapper.

Ideal conditions Incoming tide with northwesterly to northeasterly winds, or outgoing tide with southwesterly to southeasterly winds.

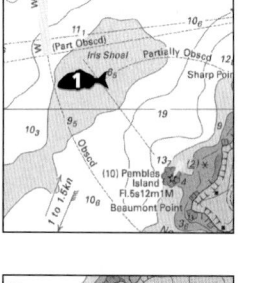

4 Mullet Point

A good longline spot: set it out on the sand, just past the foul on the eastern side.

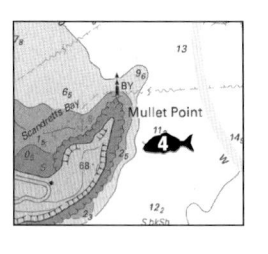

5 Rabbit Island

Massive kelp beds surround the island. Anchor just beyond casting range of the kelp line. Strayline back to the edge of the kelp and use plenty of berley and groundbait.

Ideal conditions Incoming tide with northerly winds.

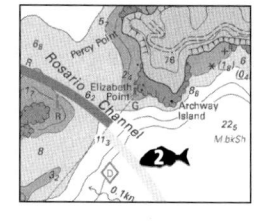

6 Middle Reef

This lies between the Mayne Islands. Use the same formula as described for Rabbit Island. The best fishing is at dusk and into the dark.

Ideal conditions Incoming tide with northerly winds.

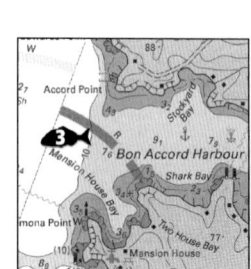

Winter

There is good straylining here close to the shore right through the winter. Although there are seldom any very big fish, 1–2-kg snapper can be caught consistently using berley and groundbait. If there are any big snapper around, they usually cannot resist a whole fresh piper.

Passage Reef

This finger of reef extends northeast, creating a large target area back to the main rock. Strayline back into the foul with plenty of berley and groundbait.

Ideal conditions Incoming tide with southerly to southeasterly winds.

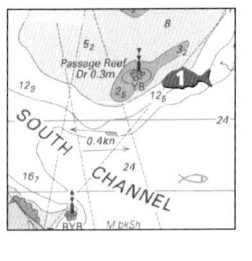

Albert Shoal

Another very overlooked area that consistently holds fish. Use plenty of berley as it will drift back and bring the fish to your baits. Be patient as it can take time for the snapper to come on to the bite.

Ideal conditions Incoming tide with easterly to southeasterly winds, or outgoing tide with northwesterly to northeasterly winds.

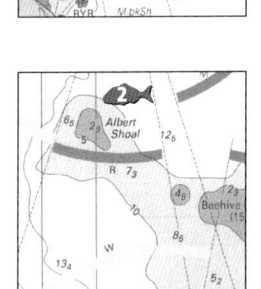

Pembles Island

Fish back to the shoreline from the middle of the island so that the berley trail surrounds the whole island.

Ideal conditions Incoming tide with northwesterly to northerly winds, or outgoing tide with southwesterly to southerly winds.

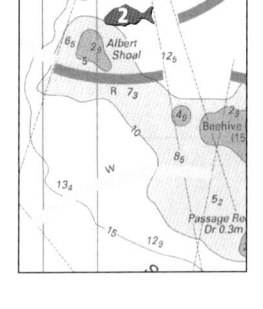

North Cove Rock

This marked rock is on the southern side of North Cove and is also a good place for kingfish.

Ideal conditions Incoming tide with northerly to northwesterly winds.

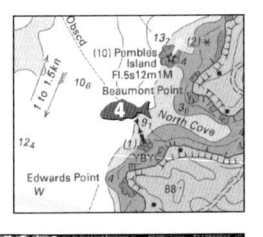

North Cove Rock

Motuketekete Island

There is a large rock off the point at the northeastern end of the island. Anchor so that the tide takes your berley and groundbait around and past the rock, and through the channel between the rock and the island. Strayline through the tide.

Ideal conditions Outgoing tide with westerly to northwesterly winds.

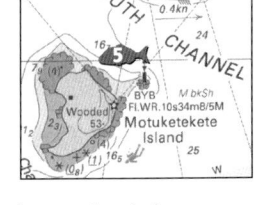

Area  Kawau to Whangaparaoa

Habitat

This area consists largely of small rocky areas of shoreline and sandy beaches, the largest of which is Orewa. There are only a few outcrops of rocks or reefs and the bottom is very muddy in places owing to the build-up of silt from local rivers. Mahurangi Harbour is a large area of shallow water and mudflats with a number of streams feeding into it. It is therefore full of crabs, shrimps and shellfish, some of the snapper's favourite foods. There are a number of islands from Kawau to Whangaparaoa and, although they have varying types of coastline, all feature kelp and provide a good habitat for snapper.

Huaroa Point, Whangaparaoa

Caution: not to be used for navigation.

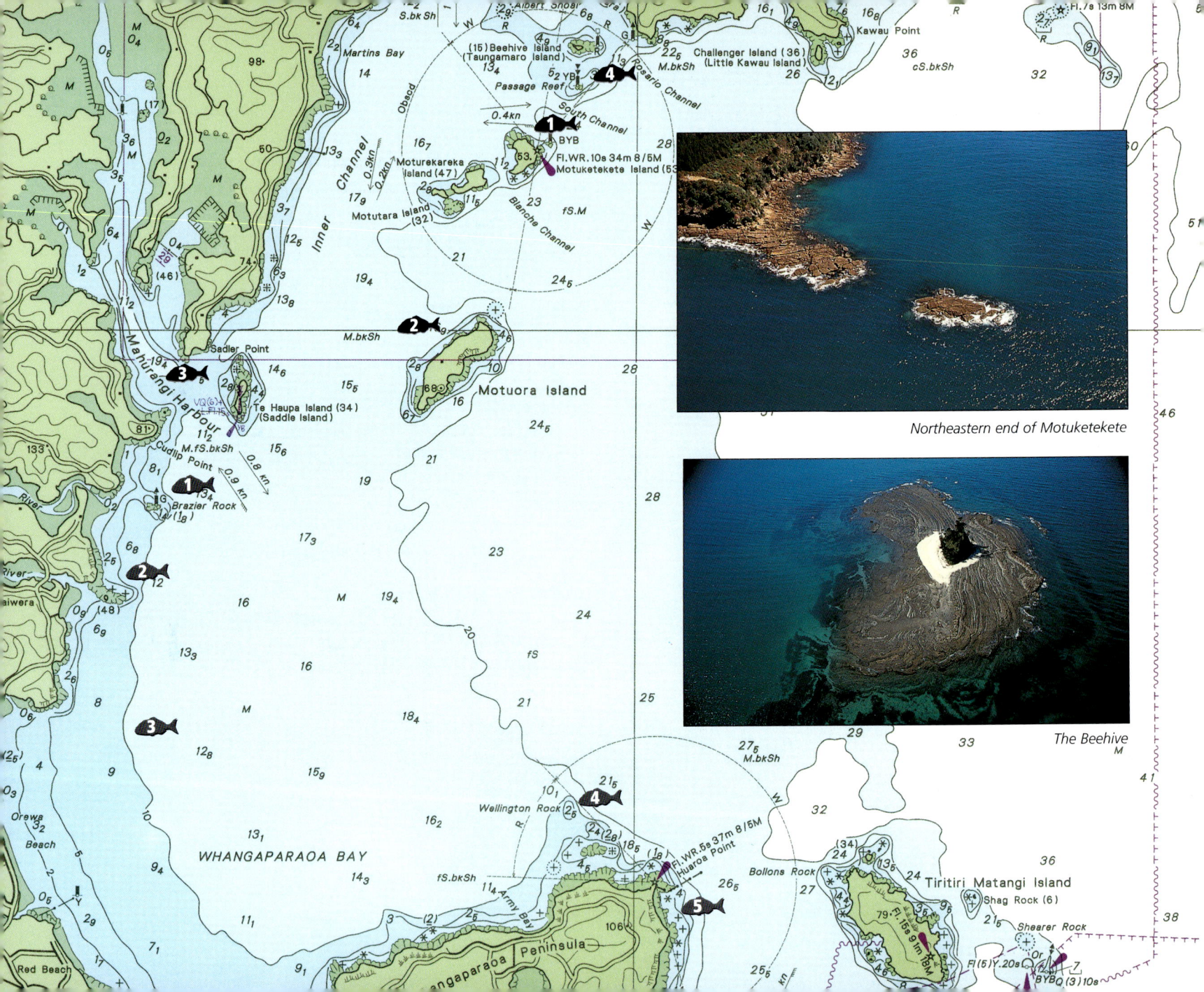

Northeastern end of Motuketekete

The Beehive

Summer

Spawning snapper tend to arrive around late October or early November and feed in deeper water (23–28 m). As the water warms, they start to feed in the shallower water (12–16 m) towards the mainland. This area is often the scene of large work-ups of baitfish that can literally last for hours. These long-lasting work-ups are like a dinner gong for the snapper, which hang around below feasting on the scraps. Jigging can be an effective way to target these snapper: slowly lower the jig until it is near the bottom (to get through the kahawai) and then work it. Speed-wind the jig to the surface occasionally in case there is a kingfish in the work-up. A longline can be a good way to discover what depth the snapper are in and what bait they prefer, as well as helping you build a database of local knowledge for the future.

 South Channel

Fish back up the rise (from 24 m to around 16 m) that lies midway between Motuketekete Island and Passage Reef.

Ideal conditions Incoming tide with easterly to southeasterly winds.

2 Motuora Island

There is a 16-m contour line running the length of the northwestern side of the island. This is a good place to drift fish as the tide direction or flow makes little difference as long as the wind is from the northeast or southwest.

Ideal conditions Any tide with northeasterly or southwesterly winds.

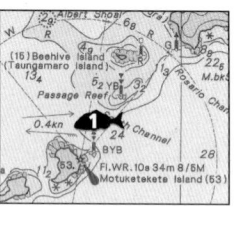

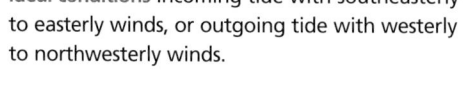

3 Mahurangi Heads

There is a finger of water (at 11–19 m) in the main channel just inside the Mahurangi Heads. Often overlooked, this area requires constant berley and groundbait and is best fished at dawn or dusk. Cast the line well back from the boat and use only just enough weight to get down to the bottom.

Ideal conditions Incoming tide with southeasterly to easterly winds, or outgoing tide with westerly to northwesterly winds.

4 Rosario Channel

In summer a lot of boats dredge for scallops in this channel, stirring up the bottom. At dusk, snapper come into the channel to feed on the ploughed-up seabed and either anchoring or drift fishing can be very productive.

Ideal conditions Incoming tide with south to southwest winds, outgoing tide with north to northwest winds.

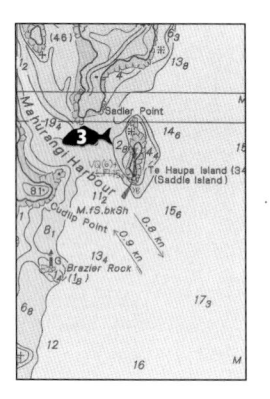

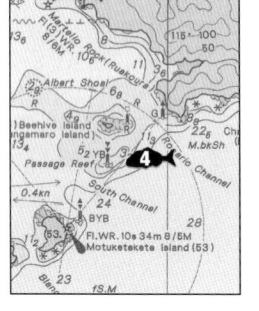

Winter

Because there is a good supply of food here, resident fish winter over around the shorelines of both the mainland and the islands, as well as in Mahurangi Harbour. Like most winter snapper they are shy, and so this area can be hard to fish at times — again, lots of berley and groundbait are required. Try fishing the 'dirty water' just beyond one of the river mouths after a big storm or very heavy rain. Snapper (particularly big ones) know that when rivers are in flood they provide a smorgasbord of snails, wetas and worms, and they feed aggressively in the stirred-up waters.

1 Brazier Rock

This rock extends underwater further than most people think and fishes well from either side. A good berley trail will go right around the structure, pulling fish back to your baits.

Ideal conditions Incoming tide with northwesterly to northeasterly winds (north side), or outgoing tide with southerly to southwesterly winds (south side).

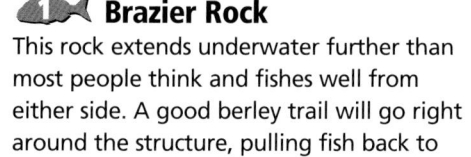

2 Mahurangi Island

A reef runs east from the island all the way to the shore and holds fish right along its edge. Anchor a little way out and draw the fish to you with berley and groundbait.

Ideal conditions An incoming tide with northwesterly to northeasterly winds is best, or an outgoing tide with southwesterly to southerly winds.

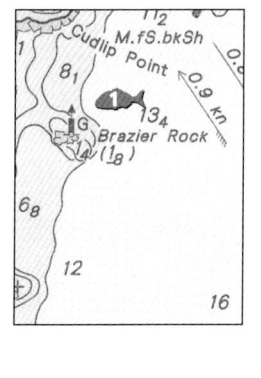

3 Whangaparaoa Bay

Longlining in this wide expanse of open area during the winter covers your bases as well as teaching you about fish movements and feeding habits.

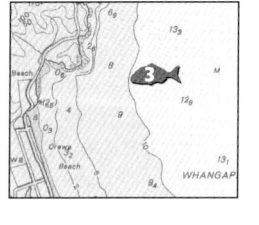

4 Wellington Rock

There is some wonderful snapper habitat between Wellington Reef and the shore, with submerged rocks, deep gutters and plenty of kelp for berley and groundbait to drift through. There are strong back eddies, especially on an outgoing tide, so those without lots of local knowledge will need to use a chart, their eyes and lots of common sense to fish the area safely. Many boats have come to grief here, usually when a big swell is running, so take care.

Ideal conditions Incoming tide with northwesterly to northeasterly winds.

5 End of Whangaparaoa

There is lots of broken foul and kelpy gutters at the very northern end of the Whangaparaoa Peninsula. Choose a spot where the wind and tide will hold the boat in a good position (see 'Straylining', page 26) and strayline through the whole tide using lots of berley and groundbait.

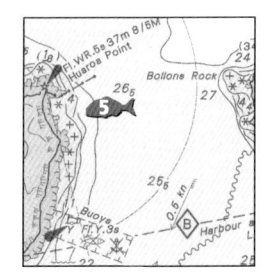

Ideal conditions Incoming tide with northerly to northeasterly winds, or outgoing tide with southeasterly to easterly winds.

Area ㉒ Tiritiri Matangi

Habitat

About two miles east of Whangaparaoa lies Tiritiri Matangi , known simply as 'Tiri', an island wildlife sanctuary that is open to the public. Tiri is surrounded by relatively deep water with a muddy, sandy bottom and a number of rocky outcrops and reefs to the east. Although the deep water comes in close to the rocky shoreline, care is needed when manoeuvring in the shallows. Lots of water flows past the island with each tide, bringing with it a steady flow of nutrients — ample food for the large schools of baitfish that live year round in these waters. In summer, large numbers of kingfish and John Dory can be caught as they gorge themselves on these baitfish. The heavily kelped shoreline contains mussels, crabs, limpets and snails, providing a great year-long habitat for snapper. That said, the summer school fish are the easier to target. The current flows fast through here, so take care when there is a strong wind blowing against the tide as it can get very rough.

Wooded Island

Caution: not to be used for navigation.

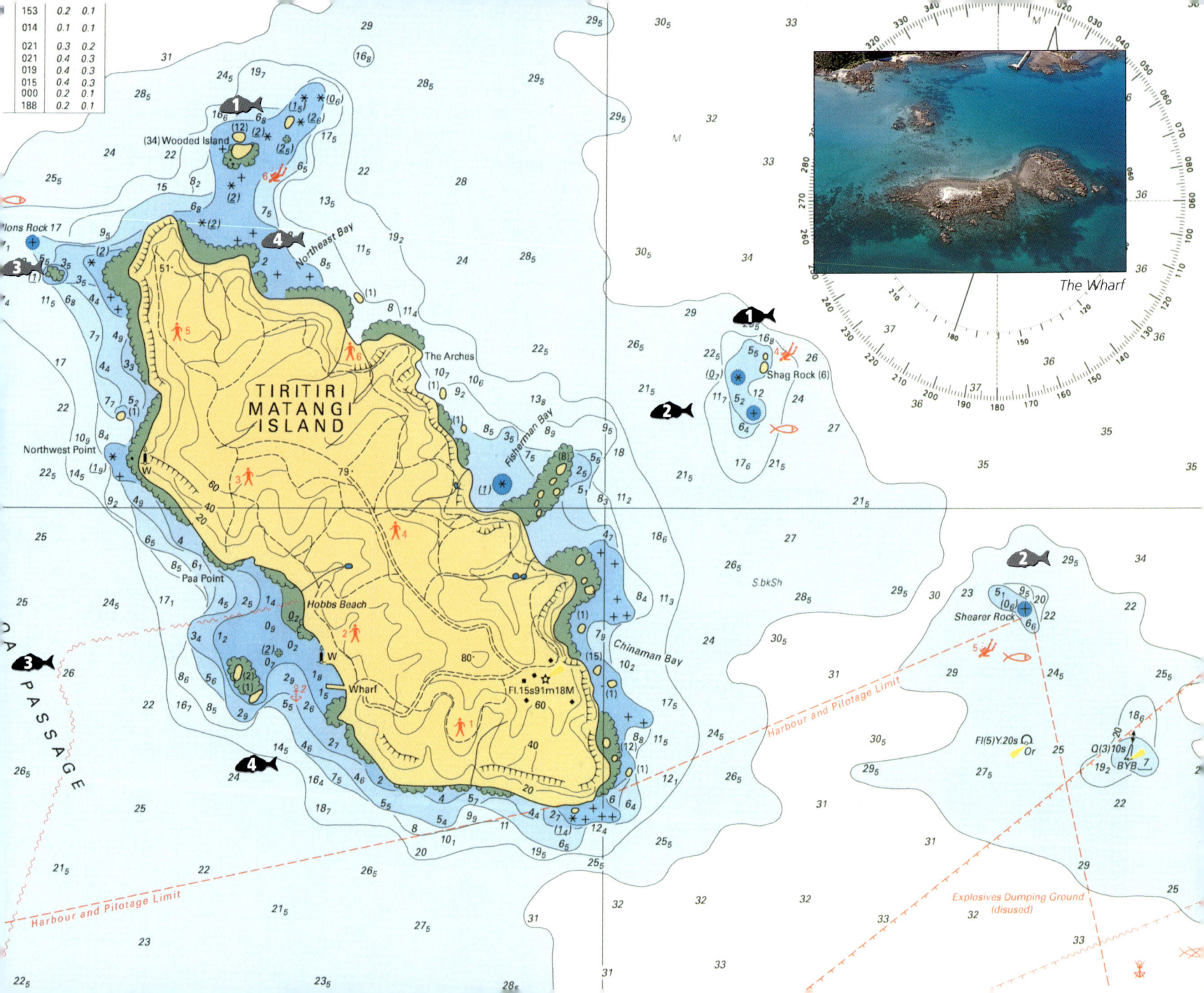

The Wharf

Summer

Pre-spawning snapper arrive in the deep water close to the island as early as September and feed around the 30-m mark. By late October, the snapper schools are found in the faster-flowing waters of the Whangaparaoa Passage (if they are slow to come on the bite, try moving to an area where the tide run is much stronger). Drift fishing using baited ledger or flasher rigs on the drop-offs around the headlands of the island can also be very effective.

1 Shag Rock (1)

There is good fishing at the northern end of the rock where the bottom rises from 29 m to 16 m. Anchor so that you can fish back up the rise.

Ideal conditions Incoming tide with northwesterly to northerly winds.

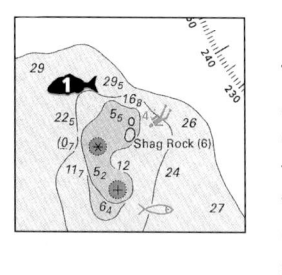

2 Shag Rock (2)

Between Shag Rock and Tiri is an area at a depth of 21.5 m. School snapper pass through here and a running sinker rig with a long trace works well.

Ideal conditions Incoming tide with northeasterly to northerly winds, or outgoing tide with southwesterly to southeasterly winds.

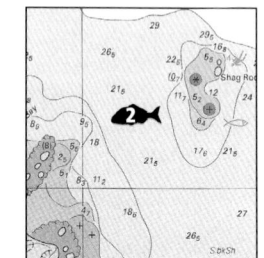

3 Whangaparaoa Passage

This is a wide expanse of fast-flowing water and can be full of snapper. Set the sounder on zoom and slowly criss-cross the area, testing possible signs by using ledger or flasher rigs. School snapper often move quickly through this area, so move uptide to see what's coming before you anchor.

Ideal conditions Incoming tide with northerly to north-northeasterly winds, or outgoing tide with southerly to southwesterly winds.

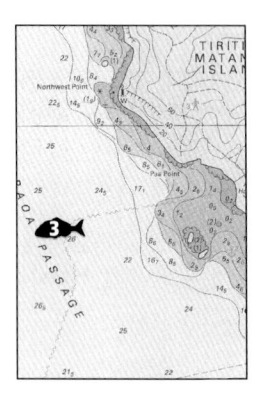

4 Bruce's Spot

Southwest of the wharf, the bottom drops from 14.5 m to 24 m and, from late November through until February, this area can hold lots of 3–4-kg snapper. However, this spot can fire for a day or two at a time and then be quiet for a week; nevertheless, it is high on the 'look at first' list.

Ideal conditions Incoming tide with northwesterly to northerly winds, or outgoing tide with southwesterly to easterly winds.

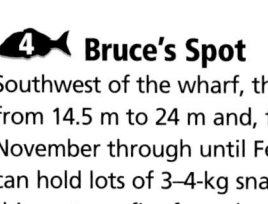

Shag Rock

Winter

The whole island and its offshore reefs and rocks can provide exciting winter fishing. However, patience is needed and it is best to set a game plan, choose a spot and then stay there over the whole tide (this is also a good way to learn about the area). A lot of the summer spots can also fish just as well in the winter. There are so many islets, submerged rocks and reefs here that virtually anywhere can be a good spot if the conditions are right. Instead of returning to the same old spots over and over again, try somewhere new and expand your local knowledge.

🐟 The Northern End

At the northern end of Tiri, around Wooded Island, is a group of rocks (some of them awash). Properly dispersed berley and groundbait (see 'Berley and Groundbait', page 32) will flow through all of the gutters and channels, attracting fish from throughout the area. This spot fishes very well after a big northerly storm.

Ideal conditions Incoming tide with northerly winds.

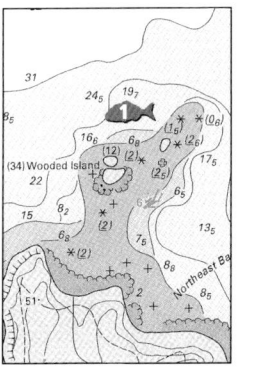

🐟 Shearer Rock

Deep water comes close in to the rock's eastern side and it is best to anchor just north of the 9.5-m line so that the berley trail and groundbait disperse at a range of depths. Big butterflied baits or whole piper stand a good chance of hooking a big snapper here. The southern side is best fished with the stern of the boat positioned just to the west of the rock so that your baits land near the rock and the reef to the west.

Ideal conditions Incoming tide with northwesterly winds (northern side), or outgoing tide with southerly to southwesterly winds (southern side).

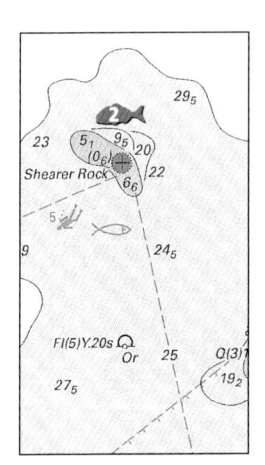

🐟 Bollons Rock Reef

Just south of Bollons Rock is a reef that can fish exceptionally well at dusk, especially after around four hours of berleying and groundbaiting. Anchor in the area over a depth of between 11.5 m and 6.8 m, about 100 m back from the foul, and cast the baits so they land just short of the foul. A big monster bait is well worth a shot here.

Ideal conditions Outgoing tide with southwesterly winds.

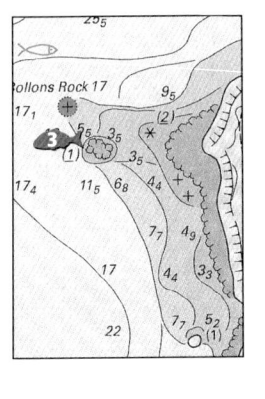

🐟 Northeast Bay

This particularly rugged area is like a supermarket, thanks to all the food living in the kelp. Use plenty of groundbait and berley and big fresh baits for a good chance at an old moocher.

Ideal conditions Incoming tide and north to northeast winds.

Heli-fishing

Heli-fishing is a great way to experience a totally different type of fishing in an otherwise impossible-to-get-to location. At the same time, you can also sharpen up your skills with expert help and have the chance to catch some really big snapper.

Introduced to New Zealand in the early 1980s by Heletranz, heli-fishing initially attracted dedicated anglers who were after trophy fish and the chance to do a little bragging. These days, heli-fishing offers those with smaller boats and less experience the chance to fish some of those remote spots previously available only to anglers with bigger boats and lots of local knowledge. Heli-fishing also offers a unique experience for people of all ages and fishing abilities — many of Heletranz's clients are corporate guests, a surprising number of whom have never fished before.

Heletranz provide all of the fishing equipment, the bait and a pilot who is also an experienced angler and guide. The pilot does not fish but is there solely to assist the other anglers. Pilot/guide John Haora has been with the company for four years and

The occasional monster snapper is a bonus.

Heli-fishing is a great way to experience a totally different type of fishing in an otherwise impossible-to-get-to location.

in that time has helped first-timers to rig up and cast out their first baits as well as land snapper over 14 kg (even hopping into the water with the net to ensure the big one didn't get away).

Although most of the clients enjoy the special buzz of fishing a remote rock in one of the more deserted parts of Great Barrier Island or the top of the Coromandel Peninsula, others prefer to combine their helicopter journey with a more conventional fishing trip on a boat. This increasingly popular option, called a heli-launch adventure, enables anglers to learn about new spots and to target big fish while still avoiding a potentially uncomfortable long sea voyage. When heli-launching, guests fly to the chosen location (generally Kawau or Great Barrier) where they rendezvous with an Oliver Royale 43 launch. Again, all equipment and bait is provided, along with an experienced skipper.

Although I've been fishing the Hauraki Gulf since I was a young kid, I must admit that there is nothing that excites me quite as much as a heli-fishing experience. The combination of fishing a remote outcrop of rock — usually with a sheer cliff towering majestically behind — and the chance of a really big snapper gives me a buzz that lasts for weeks. Even on those trips where a monster snapper does not figure, the experience is still well worthwhile. The

The combination of fishing a remote outcrop of rock and the chance of a really big snapper gives me a buzz that lasts for weeks.

chance to see the Gulf from above, to check out new spots and to get a whole new perspective on headlands, guts and barely submerged reefs is priceless, and often results in spectacular catches in the months that follow.

Although there is never any guarantee of big fish, the team at Heletranz reckon that straylining for resident snapper is best in the winter and spring months. However, the big fish are not there in the numbers they once were: it was once common to catch 10-kg fish on a heli-fishing trip, whereas now these fish are not caught quite as often. The biggest fish caught so far on a Heletranz trip was probably well over 16 kg, although it's hard to be accurate as, like many of the big fish caught now, it was released back into the water alive.

While the biggest fish are often caught during the winter months, there is often more action in the spring and summer — and the weather is usually warmer, too. Heletranz run three to four trips a week during their busy season (September through to February) and one or two trips a week during the rest of the year. Trips normally target the two hours before and after low tide, and a typical heli-fishing experience will last about five or six hours with four or five of those hours actually spent fishing.

Tony's Tips for a successful heli-fishing trip

Tony Monk
CEO and Chief Pilot Heletranz Ltd

1. Take warm, comfortable clothing.

2. Wear sturdy shoes.

3. Have a big breakfast before you go (if the fishing is hot, you won't want to stop to eat!).

4. Take a camera (many forget and regret it when then they get a big fish they want to release).

5. Go to the toilet before leaving (there aren't too many Porta-loos out there . . .)

6. Take a saltwater fly rod to target big ocean-going kahawai — it's heaps of fun!

7. Enjoy the experience of flying in a helicopter to an unpolluted, isolated spot; catching a big snapper will be a bonus.

8. Be sure to enjoy the view — this is a great opportunity to see the Gulf from a totally different perspective. You'll probably see dolphins, whales, schools of baitfish — and some interesting new spots to fish!

9. Low tide is best. Aim to arrive at the fishing spot two hours before low tide.

10. 'East is least': pick westerly winds for your heli-fishing experience.

11. Take a wide selection of baits 'to cover your bases'.

12. Berley hard and stay with your berley.

13. Use floating baits for the best presentation.

14. Go fishing with Heletranz, the company that introduced heli-fishing to New Zealand and the one that still does it best!

Fish Handling and Conservation

Those of us who live around the Hauraki Gulf are incredibly lucky. There aren't many places in the world where you can catch a great feed of fresh fish just a mile or so away from home and in clear sight of a major city centre.

The Hauraki Gulf's waters are relatively clean and unpolluted, and the snapper fishery seems well managed and sustainable. However, we can't take this for granted. We have to continue to look after the Gulf and we must always treat it with respect, taking only what we need and always thinking of the future. Because it is such a vast spawning ground, the Hauraki Gulf will always contain lots of young fish, especially in summer when so many people go fishing. It is vitally important that we look after these small fish, doing our best not to catch them and being sure to release those we do catch gently, giving them the best possible chance of survival.

Snapper prefer not to be handled. Always use a wet rag on fish you want to release, hold them upside-down and do not cover their eyes.

Use Big Hooks!

The easiest and best way you can guard against catching small fish is always to use big hooks — at least 7/0. While you will still catch some small snapper, they will only be lip-hooked and will be easy to release unharmed. If you use smaller hooks, the small snapper will gulp them down. A gut-hooked fish has very little chance of survival.

Size Matters

Note that you must release all fish under the legal minimum size, whether they are alive or not. At the time of publication, the legal minimum size for snapper in the Hauraki Gulf is 27 cm and anything smaller must be returned to the water immediately. This law is intended to give the snapper the chance to spawn at least once. Getting caught with an undersized snapper will cost you $250.

Releasing Fish

Being cold-blooded, snapper prefer not to be handled as the warmth of our hands can damage their skin, leaving them open to infection. Always use a wet rag on fish you want to release, hold them upside-down (they struggle a lot less like this) and do not cover their eyes. Try to remove the hook as quickly as possible and then release the fish gently into the water. Both undersized and legal fish that you release in this way will have an excellent chance of survival.

Fish for the Future

While it can be tempting to bring home as many fish as you can, it is better to limit your catch to what you need now. My basic rule is to take only what I can eat fresh. The sheltered nature of the Hauraki Gulf means that it is possible to catch a feed in virtually any weather. Add to this the fact that snapper can be caught right through the year, and it becomes clear that there is no need to hunt a limit bag every time you go out. Although the size limit is 27 cm, I rarely keep anything much smaller than 40 cm, and while my daily limit is nine fish, I rarely keep more than three or four. There is a lot of meat on a properly filleted pan-size snapper, and I find that six or eight fillets easily feed my family with enough left over for a friend or two as well.

Support the HFOs

While you and I always stick to the rules and are concerned about future fish stocks, there are a few people out there who think it is

The 10 fillets from these 'pan-size' snapper will provide a hearty meal for several people. Why take more if you don't need them?

okay to steal from the rest of us and from future generations by taking well over their limit or by keeping the undersized fish that are tomorrow's breeding stock. Honorary Fishery Officers (HFOs) are volunteers who also care deeply about protecting the resource and are prepared to do something about it. They undergo extensive training by the Ministry of Fisheries and patrol the nation's beaches, ramps and wharves, answering questions about fisheries legislation and checking for undersized or excess snapper. These people do an excellent job, giving up their evenings and weekends when they could be out fishing. So support them and co-operate with them if they wish to check your boat or fish bin — after all, they are looking after your interests and those of your children and grandchildren.

Above: Make up a slurry by mixing the salt ice with a bucket of seawater and placing it in a container such as a large chilly bin or ice-box.

Left: Kill any fish you decide to keep quickly with the iki method.

Looking After Your Catch

There is not much point in going to all the trouble of catching fresh fish and then letting them go off in the sun. Most good bait shops now sell salt ice, and this should always be carried, especially on long trips during the summer. Make up a slurry by mixing the salt ice with a bucket of seawater and placing it in a container such as a large chilly bin or ice-box. Kill any fish you decide to keep quickly with the iki method (insert a sharp knife or iki stick into the fish's brain just behind the eye) and then place it in the salt-ice slurry.

Safeguarding the Future

Stick to the limits, release the small ones, take only what you need and support the HFOs — a simple recipe for a sustainable fishery for generations to come.

Filleting Fish

Filleting snapper is relatively easy if you know what you are doing and a have a good-sized sharp knife.

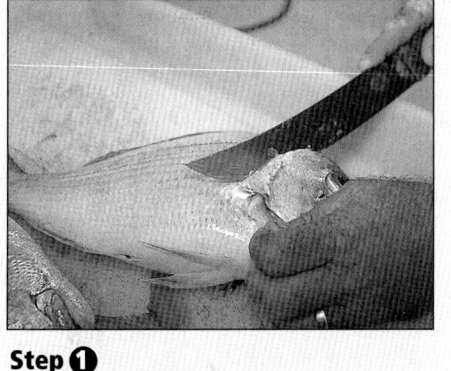

Step 1
Cut from the top of gill plate towards head.

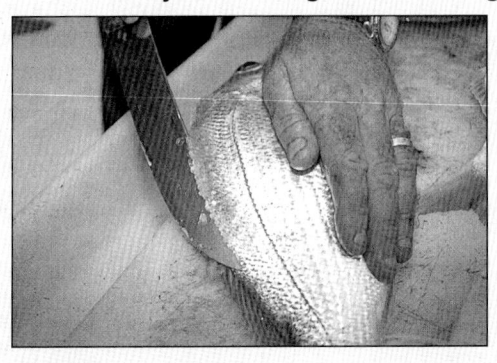

Step 2
Run the knife from the head to the tail just separating skin and flesh from fish.

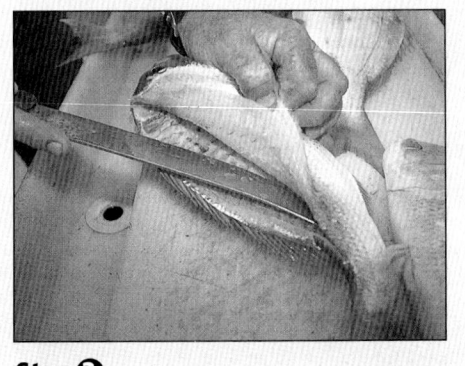

Step 3
Lift the fillet while drawing (don't hack) the knife to the head.

Step 4
Cut up and over the ribcage.

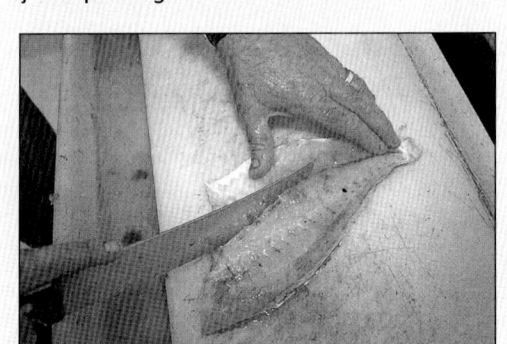

Step 5
Draw knife down either side of the bone line (don't cut through the skin).

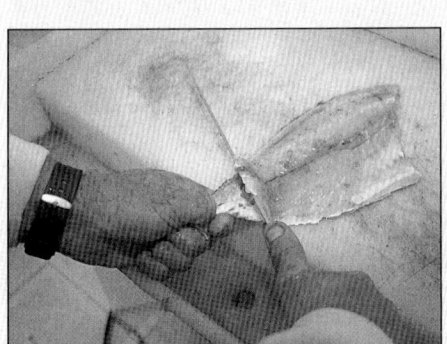

Step 6
Hold the tail end of the skin with the knife blade at 45 degrees. Pull back on the skin while holding the knife stationary in a back and forth motion until the skin is clear of the fillet.

Tips 1. Always put tail end of fillets up edge of plate to stop moisture loss.
2. Always wash hands in cold water.

MINISTRY OF FISHERIES
Te Tautiaki i nga tini a Tangaroa

Sustainable fisheries within a healthy aquatic ecosystem

MINISTRY OF FISHERIES
Te Tautiaki i nga tini a Tangaroa

Guidelines for releasing undersized fish

A guide to New Zealand's marine recreational fishing rules
Effective from 1 June 2001. Subject to change without notice

Set net Code of Practice
Effective from June 2002. Subject to change without notice

This cost him $250 at the beach
We don't want to give you an infringement fee, but from now on, if you break the fishing rules, we may.

Auckland and Kermadec Fishery Management Area
(includes Northland, Waikato and the Bay of Plenty)

MINISTRY OF FISHERIES
Te Tautiaki i nga tini a Tangaroa